Who Moved My Mouse?

Who Moved My Mouse?

A Self-Help Book for Cats
(Who Don't Need Any Help)

Dena Harris
"America's Cat Humorist"

and Mr. Nom-Noms
"America's Most Know-It-All-Expert . . . on Everything"

Illustrations by Ann Boyajian

TEN SPEED PRESS
Berkeley

For the Tall Guy

Copyright © 2010 by Dena Harris
Illustrations copyright © 2010 by Ann Boyajian

Published in the United States by Ten Speed Press, an imprint of the
Crown Publishing Group, a division of Random House, Inc., New York.
www.crownpublishing.com
www.tenspeed.com

Ten Speed Press and the Ten Speed Press colophon are registered trademarks
of Random House, Inc.

Library of Congress Cataloging-in-Publication Data

Harris, Dena.
  Who moved my mouse? : a self-help book for cats (who don't need any help) /
by Dena Harris. — 1st ed.
      p. cm.
   Includes index.
   Summary: "This self-help guide will empower cats to make the 20 minutes
they're awake each day the best 20 minutes of their lives"—Provided by publisher.
1. Cats—Humor. 2. Cats—Miscellanea. I. Title.
   PN6231.C23H29 2010
   818'.602—dc22
                                    2010008796

ISBN 978-1-58008-356-0

Printed in the United States of America

Design by Chloe Rawlins

10 9 8 7 6 5 4 3 2 1

First Edition

Contents

The secret of success is knowing who to blame for your failures.

—Author unknown (but probably a cat)

Acknowledgments

FROM MR. NOM-NOMS
First, I'd like to acknowledge my superiority and thank all of you for doing the same. That about covers it, but the human who did absolutely no work on this book except to transcribe, type, edit, and assemble it (and dole out the occasional tuna treat when inspiration ran low) wishes to say a few words as well. I can't be expected to hang around for that. Bored now. Leaving. Good-bye.

FROM THE HUMAN
It's harder than you might think to look someone in the eye and admit your latest project is a self-help book for cats. (But sometimes when you do, people feel sorry for you and give you grocery money.) Many thanks to the following feline-loving friends who not only kept a straight face when told about the book but encouraged and assisted in its creation along the way. In no particular order, paws up to Ron Culberson, Trisha Emish, Edmund Schubert, Laine Cunningham, Tom Barker, Rudy Daugherty Clark, Daniel Shirley, Pam Cable, and Christopher Laney.

Purrs and head butts to Winifred Golden with Castiglia Literary Agency for taking on the book, and for her willingness to accept and respond to email with subject lines like "Re: What do you think of this joke about cat litter?"

Many thanks to Ten Speed Press and my wonderful editor, Lisa Westmoreland.

And, finally, a special thanks to Lucy and Olivia, who remind me daily that cats are *purr*fect and don't need my help.

CHAPTER ONE

A Cat's Conversations with God

Y*ou are about to listen in on an extraordinary conversation. A conversation you may think isn't possible. . . .*

What if you were offered the chance to quiz God and ask all of the questions you've ever had about existence: why rocking chairs are allowed to exist, where the feather on a stick *really* goes when it's slid under the couch, and why your humans refuse to recognize the goldfish as sushi, for starters.

What if God answered you? (And it wasn't just the catnip talking.)

When patrolling the underside of chairs and swatting the TV remote to regions unknown fails to bring about the normal glow of satisfaction, that's when you notice the ache in your heart. Something is missing. This conversation will replace it. Heal it. Or, at the very least, it will temporarily distract you until an innocent little bird (read: afternoon snack) shows up in your yard.

Are you ready? God has something to say to you.

Dear God, what is the purpose of the dog? I've wracked my brain and all I could come up with was . . . well, nothing. Nada. Nil. No comprendo.

I have created a world of polarity. There can be no up without down, no black without white, no meows without barks. Dogs serve to maintain this polarity. For cats to be revered as elegant, refined, and superior, there must be a clumsy, crude, substandard species through which to offer a relevant comparison. Dogs serve my purpose of showcasing the feline as my highest creation.

🐾

Then why does "Dog" spelled backward equal "God"?

That was an oversight on my part. Horrible mistake. Lots of confusion resulting from that one—I'm still trying to sort it out. My apologies.

🐾

Will leaving small animal offerings on my human's back porch earn me bonus points in Heaven?

It can't hurt. Nothing says "I love you" like an unexpected gift, especially if it's still kicking. Very sweet of you to share. Good kitty!

🐾

Why do you allow bad things, like rocking chairs, vacuum cleaners, and matching pet-and-"owner" outfits, to exist?

A lot of that sort of thing is for my own amusement. I still get a chuckle about the "carry a Chihuahua in a purse" trend I instigated. I can't believe people fell for that one.

Yes, but what about those rocking chairs? They really hurt.

Did I not give you lightning-fast reflexes? They're meant to compensate for the dangers found in this world. Pull out those claws and show that rocking chair who's boss.

I'm trying to attain nirvana. Are fifty sessions of bottom licking a day enough to produce inner peace?

Not quite. But you're close. Keep going.

Why does no one understand my vendetta against the couch tassels? They are evil and must be destroyed.

Don't worry what others think. Instead, rest assured that when you attack a random object—especially one with fringe—you are doing God's work.

Why do cats see better than people do in the dark?

I thought it would be funnier that way.

So where does that feather on a stick really go when people slide it underneath the couch? I'm afraid to stick anything more than my front paws under there.

Even I'm not sure where the darkness under the couch leads, but I've been told that it empties out somewhere near Vegas.

In regard to fish tanks, how long before I'm allowed to, um, play with the fish in there?

If I catch you anywhere near the fish tank, I'm getting out the squirt gun. And, being God, my aim is quite good. Understood?

Gotcha. How about this: Why nine lives? Why not seven or twelve or thirty-six?

Nine lives matched the brand of cat food already on the market. It seemed logical.

Is gluttony a sin? (There's no reason I'm asking. Just curious.)

I'll say this: Mealtimes should *not* resemble sharks swarming around chum thrown in the water. Instead, you should pause (or paws—hee hee—get it?) to offer thanks for the nourishment you receive. Is gobbling your food a sin? No. Is it a little gross to watch? Frankly, yes.

Do black cats really bring bad luck?

No, but don't tell. Black cats are having a lot of fun messing with people on this one.

Why do people insist on picking me up when I want my feet to remain firmly on the ground?

There's an obvious lack of communication. Try sinking your claws into the person's chest and see if that clears up the misunderstanding.

I'd be interested in hearing your opinion on whether cats should be kept indoors, outdoors, or a combination of the two.

I've learned to never discuss religion, politics, or the indoor/outdoor cat debate with those I wish to keep as friends. I will say, though, that it would help resolve the issue if your species were more decisive about whether you *want* to be in or out. Because meanwhile you're letting in a whole lot of flies.

Why do I like catnip so much?

It's a little-known fact that catnip is 5 percent Viagra, 10 percent oyster extract, and 85 percent Red Bull.

Why do I keep racing from room to room for no apparent reason?

See previous question.

Why do people spew baby talk at me?

The eleventh commandment, which forbids anyone from uttering a sentence containing more than five words starting with a *w* (for example, "What a cute widdle cat wid da widdle face and whatsuh kiddy doing wid his widdle paws") was inadvertently left off the list. I could fix it now, but why bother? And really, it's not humans' fault. I just made you too darn cute. Didn't I? Yes, I did. Yes, I did. You widdle cutie-pie. Oh—ahem. Sorry.

Is there something wrong with me that I enjoy rolling around in dirty socks, bras, and underwear?

Not unless you start wearing them.

How come no one has ever been able to figure out where exactly a purr comes from?

I'm waiting for my patent to go through before I release that information.

Why do the cats on TV appear to be enjoying life so much more than I am? I don't seem to experience the same level of rollicking fun and satisfaction in my litter box as they do in theirs.

Remember that most of what you see on TV isn't real. (Except for pro wrestling. You just can't fake that kind of thing.)

🐾

I read somewhere that the earth revolves around the sun, but I was positive that the world revolved around me. What's the truth?

I know how much you enjoy the sun, so that's why I made the earth revolve around it. No worries. It all still comes back to you in the end.

🐾

Do you answer prayers?

Of course. Remember when the Doberman next door experienced that unfortunate incident with the Garden Weasel? Coincidence? I think not.

🐾

My humans yell at me when I eat food that's been dropped on the floor. Do they have a point? Is it unsanitary?

Not as long as you follow the five-second rule. Who do you think invented that, anyway?

🐾

If people don't want me on the computer, then why did they give it a mouse?

Just another example of the mixed messages you receive from humans. It's like when they chide you for sharpening your claws on the sofa. Hel-*lo*. Why did they put the sofa there to begin with?

⚫

Whom do you consider to be the unsung heroes of the world?

Animal rescue volunteers, Fancy Feast factory workers, and the inventor of salmon-flavored Greenies Pill Pockets.

⚫

Good list. Anyone else?

I've always thought that William Shatner has never really gotten his due as an actor.

⚫

Why are dogs considered loyal and cats standoffish? It's not fair.

I had to do *something* to give dogs a chance. You have brains, beauty, wit, grace, and silent paws that allow you to sneak up on people. All dogs have are bad breath, overactive saliva glands, and a lack of personal boundaries. Loyalty was my way of throwing canines a bone, so to speak.

⚫

Who started the myth that a cat always lands on his or her feet?

This guy named Phil around 1200 BCE.

☙

Why do smelly shoes—especially leather—hold such fascination for me? I can't leave them alone.

I'm not entirely comfortable discussing this. I'll give you the number of my therapist.

☙

God has a therapist?

Unfortunately, there aren't enough cats in the world to calm my nerves after a day spent dealing with people who insist on mucking up my planet. Wars, pollution, low-rise jeans . . . I've got my hands full.

☙

Why do humans insist on rubbing my fur the wrong way?

For the same reason they insist on watching reruns of *The Golden Girls* and listening to disco. They're insane.

☙

Here's a question. Did curiosity really kill the cat?

No. The original phrase is actually "Ferocity filled the rat," but it got messed up in one of those "telephone" games.

☙

*What's the deal with our lack of opposable thumbs? It's like you
don't want us to be able to work doorknobs or open pop-top cans
on our own.*

There was a coin toss. Humans got opposable thumbs, and cats
got whiskers that pick up seventy-six radio frequencies, tails
that aid in balance, and the land-on-your-feet thing. Frankly,
I think you came out ahead.

.   🐾

Why is it that no one appreciates my lightning-fast ninja skills?

I'm not sure, but your leaping out of the shadows screaming,
"Aaahhhiiii-yaaay!" each and every time you attack a dust
bunny doesn't help matters.

🐾

*I've held this conversation with you while looking at myself in the
hallway mirror. Does that mean I am God?*

Pretty much, yes.

🐾

❖ CHAPTER TWO ❖

*Purr*sonality Profile

Are you a type A feline, driven to roam at night and forever worrying when the kibbles run low? Are derogatory epithets such as "Lazy Furball" being continually thrown your way (when you're awake to hear them, that is)? What if you learned that your penchant for digging in the litter or eating plants was predestined? In other words, what if nothing you do is ever your fault?

*Purr*sonality type affects everything in a feline's life, from stalking tendencies to catnip addictions, from sleeping habits to social interactions. The test that follows identifies innate *purr*ferences. Once you complete the test, you'll identify yourself as one of sixteen *purr*sonality types. Please note that, just as there is no right or wrong way to decapitate a chipmunk, there is no or "best" or "worst" type.

Knowing your type will enable you to better express your natural *purr*ferences in daily life. You'll identify careers you may find interesting, and you'll learn how to compensate for any fur-raising quirks you may have. An SEBR (Snuggler Eager Bold Rebel) cat, for example, can become overstimulated and make poor decisions based on what is happening in the moment ("I will climb to the top of this cool tree!"), rather than pausing to see the big picture ("I am potentially stuck in this tree for all eternity").

After completing the profile, you can use it for the following purposes:

- Identify strengths (yours) and weaknesses (others).

- Determine how much social interaction you can stand before you start shredding furniture.

- Find your ideal personality match for an indentured servant (in other words, person).

- Answer questions such as "Aaugh! Why did you do that?" and "What on earth is the *matter* with you?!"

- Identify ideal occupations for your type, such as sleep study participant (LCFI) or undercover (literally) spy (SEBI).

- Line the litter box.

Your Profile

The profile takes approximately ten minutes to complete—or, with nap time factored in, three days.

The *cat*egories for your profile can be found on the following chart.

CATEGORY DESCRIPTIONS

Where you focus your attention	L	**Loner:** Cats who are Loners need no one and nothing (except the occasional tuna treat when absolutely *no one* is looking). Your focus is on finding remote places in the home so your humans think you have run away.	S	**Snuggler:** Who loves everybody? You do! Cats who are Snugglers focus their attention on nudging as close as possible to people, other animals, and any piece of fleece, no matter how large or small.
The way you take in information	E	**Eager:** Cats who are Eager exhibit a natural curiosity toward life. What's in the bag? Why is the bathroom door closed? What happens if I eat this plant? Inquiring minds like yours want to know!	C	**Comatose:** Is life worth waking up for? Cats who are Comatose don't even open their eyes for the doorbell. These kitties tend to take in information through the inner senses, using instinct and half-open eyelids to experience reality. If it's not on fire or something you can eat, your involvement will likely be minimal.
The way you make decisions	B	**Bold:** Cats who are Bold make decisions rashly, often without considering the consequences. Cats who throw down with Rottweilers or find themselves trapped in interior walls are usually of the Bold temperament.	F	**Fraidy-Cat:** Fraidy-Cats startle easily, are tentative in their approach to life, and feel most secure under a bed, where they spend all their time thinking of the bad things that could happen to them. Their decisions are based on the perceived threat of death and/or a bath. Leg muscles are highly developed in Fraidy-Cats, allowing vertical leaps of 3,500 feet.

| How you deal with the outer world | R | Rebel: Rebel cats know who they are, what they want from life, and how best to go about getting it! Rebels prefer using wit, cunning, and the threat of urinating in the bedsheets to persuade those around them to do their bidding. | I | Innocent: Cats who are Innocent see the best in everyone, even when they're being loaded into the cargo bin of a 747. They ask only for love and the occasional belly rub. Wide-eyed charm typically wins others over to their way of thinking. |

INSTRUCTIONS: *Please scratch one response only to complete each sentence or answer each question below.*

1. I sleep best

   a. Intertwined with other felines.

   b. On my own.

   c. Splayed across the center of the bed, pushing other occupants to the outermost corners.

   d. On top of somebody's face.

2. I play in brown paper bags because

   a. I'm not allowed near the knives.

   b. They're like my own personal "bat cave."

   c. If I can't see you, you can't see me.

   d. I enjoy the echo.

3. This cat

a. Had a novice taxidermist.

b. Was in the middle of a staring contest when something went terribly wrong.

c. Sees dead people.

d. Is going to explode if he doesn't find a litter box sometime soon.

4. I trust strangers

a. Easily—one can never have enough friends.

b. Never—for all I know, they could be dog people.

5. I believe that

a. Someday I will catch that mysterious red dot of light on the floor.

b. I will never catch the mysterious red dot of light.

c. Through teamwork, together we can catch the mysterious red dot of light.

d. The mysterious red dot of light is Satan's little helper.

6. When people pet me, my instinct is to

    a. Show them my belly.

    b. Show them my belly, and then attempt to bite and/or maim them when they try to touch it.

    c. Purr loudly.

    d. Think "Pet *me*? What, you have a death wish?"

7. This cat is thinking

    a. "Oy vey."

    b. "You did *what* with my dead bug collection?!"

    c. "I can see my bed from up here."

    d. "I thought superglue didn't stick to fur."

8. My favorite hiding place is

    a. In the clothes hamper. Mmm, stinky clothes!

    b. Whatever small, out-of-the-way space I can squeeze my plus-size figure into.

    c. Frozen in the middle of the floor. I tend to panic in the face of danger.

    d. Cleveland.

9. My emotional response to situations is usually

   a. Predictable.

   b. Varied.

   c. What's an emotional response?

10. If my human comes home smelling of another cat, I

    a. Throw myself under the vacuum. Our love is dead.

    b. Who cares? Feed me.

11. I have fallen asleep in my food dish

    a. Never.

    b. Occasionally.

    c. What? That doesn't double as a bed?

12. Which image do you prefer?

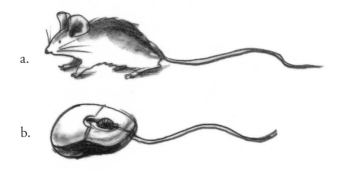

a.

b.

13. When I knead my paws on my human's belly, I'm actually

    a. Expressing pleasure.

    b. Trying to find the "self-destruct" button.

    c. Pretending to make biscuits.

    d. Seeing if I can rupture an internal organ.

14. If I suspect myself to be in the presence of someone who doesn't like cats I

    a. Urinate on his or her personal belongings.

    b. Ignore the person, and then urinate on his or her personal belongings.

    c. Make every attempt to befriend the person, and then urinate on his or her personal belongings.

    d. Sit at a distance and glare at the person, and then urinate on his or her personal belongings.

15. My favorite game is

    a. How Long Is This Unraveling Upholstery String?

    b. 3 a.m. Wake-Up Call.

    c. Stalk the Foot.

    d. Let Me In, Let Me Out.

16. This cat is thinking

   a. "I'm not coming out until I receive the 'all clear' signal."

   b. "One step closer and I weel keel you."

   c. "Laundry day, my ass."

   d. "I'll get you, my pretty, and your little dog too!"

17. My attitude toward sex is

   a. Conservative.

   b. Liberal.

   c. Gross!

   d. Not sure. Let me sit at the end of the bed and observe.

18. Complete this phrase: We have nothing to fear but

   a. The caffeine-laden Chihuahua next door.

   b. Nail clippers.

   c. Everything. We should fear everything.

   d. The cat carrier.

19. My advice to a cat who breaks something is

    a. Work the wide-eyed "who, *me?*" angle.

    b. Run away.

    c. Sprinkle pieces of the broken item near the dog's bed.

    d. Request legal counsel.

20. Which feline just regurgitated lunch in his or her human's shoe?

    a.   b.

21. When I find a dead bug, I

    a. Play a quick pickup game of street hockey with it.

    b. Pounce on it, so it appears that I made the kill.

    c. Ignore it. I have standards.

    d. Add it to my under-the-bed "Favorite Things" collection.

22. The vet exists

    a. To help me.

    b. To hurt me.

    c. Because God is testing me.

    d. To confirm my standing as the most violent patient they've ever seen.

23. Select the caption that best describes this photo.

    a. As a kitten, Tiger learned the importance of stretching before the chase.

    b. Belly rub. *Now.*

    c. It's a bird! It's a plane! It's *Supercat!*

    d. Help! I've fallen and I can't get up.

24. If something in the house is moved or changed

    a. I don't notice.

    b. I investigate immediately.

    c. Why? Why would they do that to me?

    d. It's a sign of the apocalypse. Start packing.

INSTRUCTIONS: *Slowly and stealthily circle the number that best matches your response to each statement below.*

25. If Timmy fell in the well

1	2	3	4	5

I'd *so* pull a Lassie! ———————— What's your question?

26. I am playful and outgoing

1	2	3	4	5

Every minute of ———————— Never, leave me alone
the day and night

27. I keep my kitty toys put away and organized

1	2	3	4	5

Not so much ———————————— Not my problem

28. I put the needs of others before my own

1	2	3	4	5

Always ———————————— Others have needs?

29. I prefer friends who are

1	2	3	4	5

Real ———————————— Stuffed with catnip
and come with a
manufacturer's warranty

30. When working on an important task, I tend to

1	2	3	4	5
Throw up				Fall asleep

31. Philosophical debates (such as "Which came first, the chicken or the chicken-flavored treat?") interest me

1	2	3	4	5
Not so much				Why do you ask? Do you *have* a chicken-flavored treat on you?

32. I wake my humans up early because

1	2	3	4	5
I miss them				Screw them

33. A food bowl with my name on it means

1	2	3	4	5
I'm loved				I'm humiliated—especially if it's pink

34. Time spent on personal grooming is never wasted.

1	2	3	4	5
True				Very true

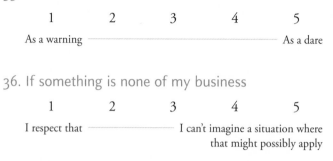

35. A hiss is meant

1	2	3	4	5
As a warning				As a dare

36. If something is none of my business

1	2	3	4	5
I respect that		I can't imagine a situation where that might possibly apply		

SCORING KEY

Assign yourself the following points for questions 1 through 24 and transfer them to the chart on the next page, along with the circled numbers from questions 25 through 36.* Then add up the points in each column to determine your *Purr*sonality Profile.

 1. a=2, b=4, c=3, d=1
 2. a=4, b=3, c=1, d=2
 3. a=1, b=3, c=4, d=2
 4. a=1, b=2
 5. a=3, b=2, c=1, d=4
 6. a=2, b=3, c=1, d=4
 7. a=1, b=2, c=3, d=4
 8. a=3, b=2, c=1, d=4
 9. a=1, b=2, c=3
10. a=2, b=1
11. a=1, b=2, c=3
12. a=2, b=1

13. a=1, b=4, c=2, d=3
14. a=1, b=2, c=4, d=3
15. a=1, b=4, c=3, d=2
16. a=1, b=3, c=2, d=4
17. a=1, b=2, c=4, d=3
18. a=4, b=3, c=1, d=2
19. a=2, b=1, c=4, d=3
20. a=1, b=2
21. a=2, b=3, c=4, d=1
22. a=1, b=2, c=3, d=4
23. a=2, b=3, c=4, d=1
24. a=3, b=4, c=2, d=1

* *Give yourself 5 points for every question you couldn't be bothered to answer. Give yourself 50 points if you decided to shred this quiz and just watch Dr. Phil instead. (What is it about that man?)*

COLUMN A	COLUMN B	COLUMN C	COLUMN D
1.	2.	3.	4.
5.	6.	7.	8.
9.	10.	11.	12.
13.	14.	15.	16.
17.	18.	19.	20.
21.	22.	23.	24.
25.	26.	27.	28.
29.	30.	31.	32.
33.	34.	35.	36.
Total for Column A:	Total for Column B:	Total for Column C:	Total for Column D:
———	———	———	———
This is your LONER/SNUGGLER score	This is your EAGER/COMATOSE score	This is your BOLD/FRAIDY-CAT score	This is your REBEL/INNOCENT score

How You Stack Up—If You Care

Now you'll plot your score on a *Purr*sonality Profile chart. For example, the *Purr*sonality Profile of a SEBI feline with the following scores would look like this:

*PURR*SONALITY PROFILE FOR SEBI
Snuggler 12   Eager 32   Bold 26   Innocent 10

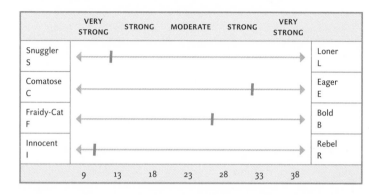

As you can see, the dominant characteristic for this feline is Innocence, coupled with a strong desire to Snuggle and be near people. Average fear and low lethargy levels indicate a cat who is happiest snooping around underwear drawers and wrestling with the dog.

Plot your own score below.

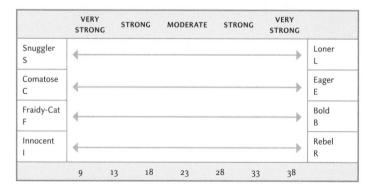

THE SIXTEEN *PURR*SONALITY TYPES

SCFR: Nurturer	LCBR: Nonconformist	SEBI: Explorer
SCFI: Visionary	LCBI: Scientist	SEFI: Comedian
LCFR: Yogi	SEBR: Disciplinarian	LEBI: Analyzer
LCFI: Romantic	SEFR: Helper	LEFI: Sensitive
SCBR: Guide	LEBR: Traditionalist	
SCBI: Trendsetter	LEFR: Compulsive	

The Sixteen *Purr*sonality Types

Your score will reflect how you manage in your day-to-day life. For example, if you get a high Fraidy-Cat score, your aversion to the doorbell, wind, and stiletto heels begins to make sense.

Scores identify *cat*titudes and behaviors common to each *purr*sonality type. To illustrate this point, we have included each type's common responses to the question "Is the food dish half full or half empty?"

SCFR/NURTURER: I want everyone else to eat—No, wait! Everyone except you, I mean!—before I go near the dish.

SCFI/VISIONARY: If we scarf down everything that's here, more might appear.

LCFR/YOGI: Whether the dish is full or empty matters not. The question is, what makes us crave food that tastes like cardboard?

LCFI/ROMANTIC: How do my humans love me? Let me count the ways. One kibble—nom, nom, nom. Two kibbles—nom, nom, nom. Three kibbles—non, nom, nom. Four kibbles . . .

SCBR/GUIDE: I know the way! Everyone follow me to the food dish!

SCBI/TRENDSETTER: Blech! That food is *so* yesterday's kibble. Engage shunning mode.

LCBR/NONCOMFORMIST: Hey! Does anyone dare me to eat out of the dog's dish instead?

LCBI/SCIENTIST: Given the components of manganous oxide, copper sulfate, and glyceryl monostearate, one must question the validity of this being classified as "food." I suspect a plot to poison us.

SEBR/DISCIPLINARIAN: This kibble had better be good or I'm gonna put da hurt on some humans.

SEFR/HELPER: Here, let me pass out utensils and moist towelettes before we begin. Did everyone wash their paws?

LEBR/TRADITIONALIST: Humph! That's not how my mom prepares my food.

LEFR/COMPULSIVE: I must chew each kibble exactly twenty-one times before swallowing. Luckily, I can fit upward of 150 kibbles in my mouth at any one time.

SEBI/EXPLORER: Forget the food! I made a seek-and-find treasure map involving the kitchen countertops, the potted plants, and the bread drawer. Who's in?

SEFI/COMEDIAN: Hey! Watch me stuff my face with kibble. Now guess what I am. A puffer fish! Get it? Get it?

LEBI/ANALYZER: It's been almost an hour since anyone has paid attention to us, so whether the dish is half full or half empty is irrelevant. What matters is that we've been left here to *die*.

LEFI/SENSITIVE: The simple beauty of the food lying scattered about the dish stirs me to the depths of my soul. Or maybe I just need to use the litter box.

CHAPTER THREE

How to Win Friends and Influence Dog People

Self-improvement guru (and probable cat lover) Dale Carnegie once said, "Believe that you will succeed, and you will." We say, "Sabotage those surrounding you, and you'll look like you're succeeding."

This chapter launches you on a voyage (sans water) of self-discovery during which you'll hone time-honored feline traits, such as stealth, sneakiness, and the ability to squeeze under recliners, that have propelled generations of cats before you to fame and fortune. Improve confidence by declaring everything in the house yours. Develop strategies to revitalize your brand and take you from house cat to glamour puss. Learn to fake an interest in others and become a sought-after conversationalist while ignoring everything that's said to you. And, most important, win people, dogs, and other lesser forms of life over to your way of thinking.

Part I: How to Win Friends

Right now you may be asking yourself, do I even want friends? Peculiar rules apply to friendship. Friends are expected to *share* (which can be defined as "to give away a portion of something

> ### Tips for Getting the Most from This Chapter
>
> - Underscore key concepts by ripping to shreds the pages on which they appear.
> - Place a hairball next to passages you wish to review at a later date.
> - Rub your scent on each page to mark your progress.
> - Promise yourself a quick snort of catnip every time you apply a principle—or even every time you *think* about applying a principle.
> - Use the side margins to record your triumphs and victories over lesser beings.
> - Nap on top of the pages and hope there's something to the idea of learning through osmosis.

that is rightfully yours without being coerced, tied up, or given a full or partial lobotomy") with other friends. This presents a problem for the average cat. Sharing was eliminated in the 1970s, when catnip-stuffed Garfield dolls burst onto the scene. Aside from the occasional Turkish tongue bath, cats have refused to share ever since.

Still, friends come in handy when you need a back scratch, a lap to curl up on, or someone to blame for the dried vomit found soldered to the living room carpet. For reasons such as these, we feel it's worth lowering your guard and allowing others to approach you for up to ten minutes daily.

How does one go about making friends? We recommend the following tried-and-true tactics:

Try blackmail. Always a strong go-to option. Figure out how to work the point-and-click camera (you'll thank us) to get the goods on others. Then threaten to upload the pictures to YouTube if they don't massage your back and neck for an hour or more.

Regift. Be it a lifeless moth, a saliva-drenched cotton mouse, or the regurgitated remnants of your lunch, a previously used gift— so long as it's from the heart (or stomach)—greases the wheels and opens the door of friendship.

Give head butts. The classic overture of friendship. They're also a good way to tell new friends to move the hell out of your way.

Go limp. Humans consider it a sign of trust when you go limp in their presence, not recognizing that you're actually feigning death in the hopes they'll leave you alone.

Provide honest feedback. Feedback is best offered late at night, when a friend's ability to throw a feather pillow in your direction with any degree of accuracy is at its lowest.

Lick a new friend. It's gross but effective. Rinse and spit after.

Mark your territory. Just as good fences make good neighbors, good scent-marking makes good friends. Don't hesitate to renegotiate boundaries and mask a friend's scent with your own.

Attack sporadically. This one's just for fun. It will arouse in your friends a nagging, persistent fear of being stalked. (Be ready with that point-and-click camera. You'll get some classic shots here.)

Take a hostage. Threaten to nap on the clean laundry until you're offered ham or tuna.

Accept a pat on the head. The head pat lets humans think you're friends; they'll never suspect they've just been targeted for annihilation.

Purr. A purr is a good, nondescript, noncommittal sign of friendship. Like "Aloha," it has many meanings, from "Hello" to "I'm going to kill you."

Claim others' possessions as your own. Drag pillowcases, underwear, or the family dog to the center of the room, plop down on them, and declare them yours. Let the bonding begin.

Bribe them with the belly. No one can resist the power of the belly. No one. Well, except for crazy Aunt Dorothy, who shows up at Christmas and smells like a kennel. But, given her love of terriers, she's one step away from the loony bin anyway.

HOW TO BECOME A SOUGHT-AFTER CONVERSATIONALIST

Once you have friends, the work isn't over. Now you're required to fake an interest in what happens to them. This is easier said than done. Feigning interest requires that you stay awake while a friend babbles on about . . . whatever it is he or she is yapping about.

Fortunately, all that will usually be required of you during a conversation is long, slow blinks to show you haven't completely lapsed into a coma. However, if you'd like to up your game, here are some tips for becoming a dazzling conversationalist.

Ask questions. Cock your head sideways and inquire, "Mrow? Mrow? Mrow?" The longer you query, the more you need to turn your head. (If you hear a crack, stop! You've gone too far.) Make a game of it and see how many "mrows" you can get in before you drive your new friend to drink.

Introduce new topics. Don't be shy about cutting someone off if you spot something more interesting to discuss, such as a dead bug on the windowsill or a piece of poo caught in your fur.

Add humor. At random points in the conversation, turn around and wave your butt in your partner's face. It's the party trick that never grows old.

Exhibit appropriate body language. A wide-eyed, steady gaze says, "I'm interested in what you have to say." A flicking tail and flat ears say, "I'm not entirely comfortable with this topic." And hiding under the bed says, "I'd rather battle dust bunnies the size of Alaska than listen to your boring stories."

Have something to contribute. Be willing to shed or cough up a hairball to get the conversation rolling.

Be curious. Curiosity is the basis of all true friendships. Investigate things that are none of your business, including medicine cabinets and odd body odors.

Part II: How to Influence Dog People

Brace yourself. There are people who prefer dogs to cats. While we're not quite sure why God doesn't just strike these unfortunates dead, we're sure he has his reasons. The good thing about dealing with dog people is that you're working with individuals who have shown themselves to be of low intelligence and questionable taste. It won't be long before you'll have them eating out of your paw.

The trick to influencing dog people—or any people, for that matter—is to make them believe that any idea you plant in their head is their own. People actually think that when they decide to offer a treat to a cat, scratch the cat's ears, or indulge their sudden urge for a tuna sandwich they are acting on their own wants and needs. They would be astounded—and more than a little frightened—if they saw the behind-the-scenes manipulation that takes place. (Tip: Pulling off the tuna sandwich trick is simply a matter of standing over your human at night and whispering in his or her ear, "Tuna, tuna, tuna, tuna, no mayo. Tuna, tuna, tuna . . .")

Dog people may try to blow you off as "just a cat." It's up to you to show them that *this* kitty has claws. In fact, the best way to get dog lovers' attention is to claw them or, better yet, eat their canary. Dog owners respect brute shows of strength. To this end, you may want to offer them a tour of your "Trail of Sorrows," including the bunny slipper you de-tailed, the napkin you surprised on the hall floor, and the loop pile rug in the bedroom that, thanks to you, will never bother anyone again.

You'll want to reward dog people for appropriate behavior. This is known as behavior modification. For example, every time a dog owner ignores his or her dog in favor of you, offer a friendly

BONUS: Six Strategies to Transform Yourself from House Cat to Glamour Puss

1. Glamour is all about *cat*titude. Believe you are all that and a bag of catnip, and others will believe as well.

2. House cats sulk, but glamour gals can work a pout as well as any emaciated supermodel. Practice your pout in a mirror until you achieve that perfect combination of indignation, hurt feelings, and whisker quiver.

3. Never put the needs of others before your own. If you're guilty of this behavior, stop it. Immediately.

4. Shed low self-esteem. Luckily, low self-esteem is carried in excess fur. Shed hair all over the house and be amazed as your confidence level skyrockets.

head butt and wind your way around his or her neck and lap. As said canine companion watches, aghast, wrap the person in a cloud of cat hair while purring, "Dogs drool, cats rule," in his or her ear. Shoot the dog "the claw" behind the human's back while you do this. Dogs are so clueless—he'll think you're saying he's number one.

At this point, your work is done. You may begin the evil purr and start licking yourself to enact the "I touched something that touched a canine" decontamination process.

5. Buy yourself a collar with bling. Nothing screams glamour like "Kitty" spelled out in fake rhinestones.

6. Strike a pose. You can vogue with the best of them. Raise a leg, stretch a paw, flip upside down, and hold it. If you have a fluffy white afghan to loll about on, all the better. Strut your stuff. They don't call it a catwalk for nothing.

CHAPTER FOUR

Who Moved My Mouse?

An Amazing Path to Declare
Revenge on Those Who Dare
Disturb What Is Yours

The short, simple parable that follows will open your eyes (seriously—wake up) to the secrets of dealing with change, stress, and indoor dogs.

In this story, Fat Cat's favorite toy is missing and everyone is suspect! Two humans, Dim and Witted, along with their canine colleagues, Dumb and Butt, put their lives on hold to join Fat Cat in his search for Mr. Mouse.

Mr. Mouse, of course, is a metaphor for what cats want in life—be it full bellies, unconditional love, or fifteen minutes alone in a dark room with a baseball bat and the stupid gerbil in his exercise wheel who thinks he owns the place. The house is where cats search for what they want—mainly because those overprotective humans won't let them outside—and the friends helping Fat Cat on his journey of self-exploration are, of course, expendable.

Enjoy this classic tale of one-upmanship, appropriate for kittens through senior cats.

"Noooo!" yelled Fat Cat. A volcano of old sock monkeys and catnip balls erupted across the room as Fat Cat dug frantically through his toy chest. Upon hitting bottom, his large black-and-white head popped up over the edge of the chest. "He's gone!"

"Who's gone?" asked Dumb, pausing to sniff a catnip ball. Being a bassett hound, Dumb sniffed everything.

"Maybe Fat Cat is gone," suggested Butt, rolling onto his back and admiring the silky Labrador fur on his belly.

"How could Fat Cat be gone?" asked Dumb. "He's sitting right there."

"Oh, right," said Butt. "Hey, when's breakfast?"

"Would you two shut up?" snapped Fat Cat. "My Mr. Mouse is gone and you're both prime suspects. You! Dumb! Quick—where were you this morning between the hours of 2 and 4 a.m.?"

"You know, Fat Cat, my name is actually Fred," said Dumb.

"Don't change the subject," said Fat Cat. "What did you and the drooling wonder do with my Mr. Mouse?"

"Fat Cat, I don't have Mr. Mouse," said Dumb. "I haven't touched it since the time I tried to nuzzle it and you dropped my rawhide bone in your litter."

"Listen," said Butt. "I hear footsteps. That means breakfast!"

Sure enough, two pairs of human feet appeared in front of the animals. They belonged to the animals' humans, Dim and Witted.

"My goodness, what a mess you've made in here," said the woman, Witted, to Fat Cat. "What are all your toys doing outside your toy box?"

"Mrow-mrow-meow!" said Fat Cat, jumping out of the box. He decided to communicate the seriousness of the missing

Mr. Mouse situation. Standing on his hind legs and clawing at Witted's robe, he added a wailing and emphatic "Mrowwwr-llll!"

"Let's get this cleaned up then, shall we?" Witted began placing toys back in the chest.

"Is she deaf?" asked Fat Cat. "I just explained Mr. Mouse is gone. Why isn't she calling 911? Is a SWAT team on the way or what?"

"I like to swat things," said Butt. "I am an excellent swatter."

"It would help if someone swatted some sense into you," said Fat Cat. "I can see I'll have to solve this crime on my own. But mark my words," he said, pausing to rub his head on the nearest door frame, "I will find Mr. Mouse, and whoever took him will come to rue the day!"

Fat Cat then gave a laugh meant to sound like "Bwa-ha-ha!" but which ended up sounding more like "Brraaack—aaaaccck!" as he coughed up his morning hairball. Undeterred, he set forth on his quest, pausing only briefly at his favorite sunbeam for an energizing two-hour nap.

The Search Begins

The search for Mr. Mouse began later that very morning with a mandatory all-pet meeting in the toy room. Fat Cat demanded that the upstairs be searched. He instructed the dogs to investigate every corner and crevice, leaving no drawer unopened or throw rug unturned. "Find Mr. Mouse," said Fat Cat. "No food breaks. No chasing your tail. Nothing else matters. Report back to me when you're through."

"What will you be doing while we're searching?" asked Butt, biting at a floating piece of lint.

Fat Gat glared at him. "Do you think a search and rescue operation plans itself?" he asked. "I've got maps to pore over, logistics to plot, and an emergency evac helicopter to charter, and I'm waiting for the Red Cross to call me back about organizing the blood drive."

"Wait—isn't Mr. Mouse cotton based?" asked Dumb.

"The blood is for the two of you, to replace the blood I'll take out of you both if you fail to find Mr. Mouse," said Fat Cat, tail bristling. "Now go!"

Dumb and Butt raced up the stairs and into the guest bedroom. Dumb immediately began a four-corner sweep of the room, while Butt bounded onto the bed and began fighting with pillows that appeared to move when he stepped on them. Dumb sniffed dresser drawers, and Butt checked behind the drapes. Finally, they nudged open the closet door and sniffed a tube-top dress, a pair of spandex pants, and a faded Santa suit that smelled like moldy fruitcake. After twenty minutes, it was clear that Mr. Mouse was not in the vicinity.

While the dogs were upstairs, Fat Cat stared out the window and thought about Mr. Mouse. Although he didn't have a lot to say, Mr. Mouse was an excellent listener and always took Fat Cat's side in an argument. Good friends like that were hard to come by. He hoped Mr. Mouse was okay and that, wherever he was, someone was giving him his daily tongue bath. Fat Cat turned away from the window as the dogs careened back into the room.

"Report?" said Fat Cat.

"Sorry, Fat Cat," said Dumb. "No sign of Mr. Mouse. But we did discover that our humans are not as hip as we thought."

"Then we keep looking," said Fat Cat. "I will hunt down whoever took Mr. Mouse and kill them—but only after I have first batted them around and let them think they are going to escape. Then I will unexpectedly pounce and—" He paused and sniffed the air. "Butt, what did you roll in? You smell like moldy fruitcake."

Butt sheepishly slunk behind the sofa to pick red and white Santa fibers from his fur.

"Anyway," said Fat Cat, "I discovered something while I was sitting here waiting for you two."

"Oh, did you discover that piece of poo hanging from your rear?" asked Butt, peeking from behind the sofa. "I wanted to say something earlier, but I didn't know how."

Fat Cat leveled the dog with a withering glance. "*No.* I knew about the poo all along. What I realized is that Mr. Mouse makes me feel loved."

Dumb stopped licking his front paws and looked up. That wasn't the sort of statement Fat Cat usually made.

"And since Mr. Mouse makes me feel loved, it's obvious that love is external," continued Fat Cat. "Therefore, love must come from things which can be bought."

"Umm, that doesn't sound quite right," said Dumb.

"You leave the heavy thinking to me, big boy," said Fat Cat. "Here, I'll write my knowledge on the floor so you may contemplate it at your leisure."

And so Fat Cat took a piece of chalk and wrote:

THE MORE STUFF WE HAVE, THE MORE WE ARE LOVED.

"Man, that is *deep*," said Butt, emerging from behind the couch. "I'm going to go count my toys right now to see how much I'm loved. Wish me luck!" He raced away.

The Search Continues

The search for Mr. Mouse resumed after lunch. By this time, Fat Cat was seriously worried about his friend. He sent the dogs to search the master bedroom and bath, as well as the family room and kitchen. Each time Dumb and Butt came back to report that there was no sign of Mr. Mouse, the deeper into gloom and despair Fat Cat fell. It wasn't long before his morose behavior raised the attention of the people in the house.

"Why so glum?" Witted asked, stroking Fat Cat. Fat Cat sighed and kept his gaze fixed on the window. The light rain pattering down matched his mood.

"I bet I know what would cheer kitty up," said Witted. She disappeared into the kitchen and returned momentarily with a Salmon Yummy, Fat Cat's favorite snack. She waved it under his nose.

"I'm too depressed to eat," thought Fat Cat as the odor of the Salmon Yummy drifted toward him. "Still . . . I must keep up my strength to search for Mr. Mouse. It's what he would want."

Witted watched Fat Cat eat the Salmon Yummy with less than his usual lip-smacking gusto. "What's the matter?" she asked.

"Here, why don't we play with Mr. Mouse? That always cheers you up."

Fat Cat perked up at the sound of his friend's name. He hopped down from the windowsill and followed Witted from room to room, meowing eagerly at her feet as she searched for Mr. Mouse.

"That's odd," she said to Dim as she walked into their study, followed closely by Fat Cat. "I can't find Fat Cat's Mr. Mouse toy. He usually never lets it out of his sight."

The insight hit Fat Cat with the speed of a squirrel bouncing off a car fender. He raced back into the toy room, picked up his chalk, and wrote:

WHEN YOU LET GO OF STUFF YOU LOVE, BAD THINGS HAPPEN.

"What's this?" asked Dumb, as he and Butt entered the room. Both dogs collapsed on the floor, panting. It had been a long day of searching.

"This is fresh insight," said Fat Cat. "I realize now that I should have kept track of Mr. Mouse's whereabouts at all times. But I didn't, and look what's happened. He's gone!"

Momentarily overcome with emotion, Fat Cat paused to give his chest fur a few quick licks. When he could speak again, he continued, "If I've learned anything today, it's this: never let anything you love out of your sight."

Butt stood up. "Excuse me," he said in a thick voice. "I think I need some one-on-one time with my squeaky newspaper." He padded out of the room.

Dumb rolled over to look at Fat Cat. "I've always heard that if you love something you should set it free," he said.

"Yes, yes. And if it doesn't come back, hunt it down and eat it," said Fat Cat. "We're all familiar with the classics. Relax, already."

Ever obedient, Dumb did just that. He was asleep and snoring within minutes.

Midnight Musings

Fat Cat was determined not to make the same mistake twice. That evening, he carefully stockpiled all his toys and divided them into three categories. The first category was made up of items he dearly loved, like his combing brush, his cat tunnel, and all the toys he'd pilfered from the dogs over the years. The second pile was things he liked but often forgot he had, such as his catnip mat and collection of holiday-themed birds (turtledoves, partridges, and the like). The third pile consisted of items that made him want to hurt the people who had given them to him. Why, for example, would anyone think he might enjoy that big brown motorized mouse? He'd almost given himself whiplash diving under the bed the first time Dim and Witted had fired up that monstrosity.

After dinner, the dogs headed back to the toy room. Dumb and Butt knew something was up the moment they entered, mainly from the way Fat Cat popped out from behind the door and slammed it behind them.

"Darn it, Fat Cat," said Dumb. "You know none of us has figured out doorknobs yet. Now we're trapped in here."

Fat Cat had not thought of that, but he pretended not to care. He directed the dogs' attention to the three piles he had made.

"Do you see these?" he asked both dogs, pointing to the first two piles. "These are mine. Not yours. *Mine.* Don't touch them. Ever."

He stopped before the third pile of toys. "See these? These are toys I've decided I don't like and will never play with."

At this, Butt's tail began to bang against the floor. He'd been waiting for years to play with that big brown mouse.

Fat Cat grinned as if he knew what Butt was thinking. "I don't use them, and I don't like them, but you're still not allowed to touch them. Why? Because they're mine. Got that?"

A deflated Butt nodded. Fat Cat gave a smug purr.

"Fat Cat, what's this?" asked Dumb. He'd noticed a new insight chalked on the floor. Dumb read it aloud:

INTIMIDATION CAN STOP OTHERS FROM MESSING WITH YOUR STUFF.

"Oh, brother." Dumb gave a slight shake of his head, sending his jowls flapping as he walked over to where Butt stood.

"Grrrr. This is *my* part of the room. Back off! Grrrr," said Butt. He stopped and looked at Fat Cat. "Is that intimidating enough?"

Fat Cat nodded. "Not bad." He paused. "How difficult would it be for you to work up some sort of rabid lather?"

"Fat Cat, stop!" cried Dumb. "This is all wrong. Being mean and scaring people and hoarding toys won't bring back Mr. Mouse. None of this will make you feel loved."

Butt, who had been snarling, stopped and looked up. "Okay, wait," he said. "Now I am, like, *so* confused."

There was a click-click and the door swung open. A grateful Dumb hurried out of the room, followed by a confused Butt. Dim and Witted entered, Witted holding something behind her back.

"Here, sweetie," she said to Fat Cat. "Look what we bought for you." She laid a fresh-from-the-box Mr. Mouse doll at Fat Cat's feet. "Look! It's Mr. Mouse!" she exclaimed, clapping her hands in delight.

"How's that, pal?" asked Dim, scratching Fat Cat behind the ears. "All better?" They walked out of the room.

Fat Cat gave a cautious sniff. The new Mr. Mouse smelled like cardboard and chemicals, not at all like the familiar Mr. Mouse smell of salvia, cat hair, and regurgitated meals.

He gave the new Mr. Mouse a tap and jumped a mile when the toy gave a "Squeak!" in return.

"What the—" thought Fat Cat. "The old Mr. Mouse didn't talk. The old Mr. Mouse just listened. I don't like this at all. But maybe I should give the new guy a chance."

Fat Cat settled into his traditional Mr. Mouse position, which is to say he lowered his backside directly onto Mr. Mouse and lay down in preparation for a nap. But no matter how much he twisted and turned, he couldn't find a comfortable spot. Plus, the squeaking sounds from underneath his butt unnerved him.

"The old Mr. Mouse had lumps in all the right places," he thought. "This new guy is terrible!" Annoyed, he batted the new Mr. Mouse across the room. He picked up his chalk to write a new insight.

CHANGE SUCKS.
ACCEPT NO REPLACEMENTS.

Night moved in and Fat Cat curled into a ball in a corner of the toy room. He felt sad and alone. He wondered if Dim and Witted were in bed. He gave a small smile as he recalled how he and Mr. Mouse liked to curl up and sleep at the foot of their bed. Sometimes Witted would hold Mr. Mouse and run him down Fat Cat's back, pretending that Mr. Mouse was combing Fat Cat. That never failed to crack up both him and Mr. Mouse. A tear formed in his eye.

Fat Cat crept across the room toward where he'd knocked the new Mr. Mouse.

I prefer to sleep alone," he told the mouse. "But since it's your first night in a new home, I'll sleep beside you tonight. Just don't get used to it."

He curled into a ball around the new Mr. Mouse and soon drifted into a peaceful slumber.

A New Day

The next day, the hinge on the toy room door squeaked as Dumb and Butt nudged it open. The first thing they noticed was Mr. Mouse, taking in some morning sun in the eastern window with Fat Cat.

"Fat Cat, you found Mr. Mouse!" exclaimed Butt. His large tail whipped side to side in excitement.

Dumb's sharp basset hound nose told him different. "That's a new Mr. Mouse," he said. He arched an eyebrow at Fat Cat. "You okay with that?"

Fat Cat shrugged. "Let's just say I had a few more insights last night," said Fat Cat.

"Oh, no," said Dumb.

"Oh, yeah!" cheered Butt. "I've been learning so much. Tell us about these new insights."

"Well," said Fat Cat. "First let's review." He pointed to the writings on the floor. "Here's what we learned yesterday."

THE MORE STUFF WE HAVE, THE MORE WE ARE LOVED.

WHEN YOU LET GO OF STUFF YOU LOVE, BAD THINGS HAPPEN.

INTIMIDATION CAN STOP OTHERS FROM MESSING WITH YOUR STUFF.

CHANGE SUCKS. ACCEPT NO REPLACEMENTS* *UNLESS YOU CAN LICK THEM INTO SUBMISSION

"Did you change that last one?" asked Butt.

"I altered it late last night," said Fat Cat, licking his front leg. "It's quite brilliant."

"Are you kidding?" asked Dumb. "These make my fur stand on end."

Fat Cat sniffed. "Reviewing all of these, I decided that, although I will always love old Mr. Mouse, there is room in my life for new things if I decide to make room."

Dumb was dumbfounded. "That's really beautiful, Fat Cat," he said. "It can take people a lifetime to realize that everything flows in and out of our lives for a purpose, and that having the courage to make room for new and unexpected things in life can open whole new doors of personal growth and fulfillment."

"What nonsense are you spewing?" said Fat Cat. "What I'm saying—and I'll repeat it for the *slooow* learners in the class—" favoring Dumb with a sharp glance, "is that I like it when people buy me new things. The end."

"That's what you learned from all this?" asked Dumb. "That change is okay so long as people buy you stuff?"

"Pretty much," said Fat Cat. He gave the new Mr. Mouse a lick.

"I learned something," volunteered Butt.

"Thank heavens someone did," said Dumb. "What did you learn?"

"I learned that Santa suits smell like fruitcake and never to mess with Fat Cat's toys."

"Excellent, Butt," purred Fat Cat. "I hope you also learned to stay away from my food dish."

"Your food dish has nothing to do with the last twenty-four hours!" exclaimed Dumb.

"I know. That's why I'm bringing it up now," said Fat Cat. "Touch it and suffer the consequences."

"Wow, I'm feeling smarter already," said Butt.

From the far corner of the toy room, wedged behind a bureau, a pair of shiny black button eyes observed the bickering animals. The original Mr. Mouse wedged himself even further back in the shadows. It had taken months of planning to escape the clutches of the evil kitty. If he never had another one of those disgusting tongue baths, it would be too soon. He felt bad for the brave comrade who had replaced him, but he couldn't risk helping him. It would take all his energy to enact Operation Sneak Out of the House Undetected.

Mr. Mouse had observed all the activity over the past day, and he knew Fat Cat had been right about one thing: change was scary. But maybe one day change would work in his favor. Maybe it would even throw a Mrs. Mouse or, better yet, some cheese his way. Until then, he would take a catnap and bide his time, as he waited and watched for the perfect opportunity to take the next step into his future of freedom.

The End ❧

Don't Sweat the Small Stuff . . . But Feel Free to Freak Out Over Anything That Moves Suddenly or Without Warning

Too often, it's the little things in life—half-digested hairballs, reruns on *Animal Planet*, claws that just don't draw blood—that has kitties wailing the alley-cat blues. But before you bury your hopes for a brighter future alongside the dog's favorite toys in the backyard, take pause. By making only small, daily changes, you can improve your life. Ratchet down stress by following simple strategies such as "Become an Early Riser—and Force Others to Join You," or "Stare into Strangers' Eyes and Smile (Unblinking, until You Break Them)." The following twenty calm-inducing strategies will leave even the friskiest feline feeling soothed, pampered, and ready to face the world with an improved *cat*titude toward life.

1.

Practice Random Acts of Kindness

Practicing small, random acts of kindness is a wonderful way to stay grounded and grateful for the many blessings made available to you in life. What does a random act of kindness look like? Treat yourself to Fido's canned food. Take some of Grandma's yarn and secret it away for a rainy day. Position yourself right in the middle of the bed at night so your humans are forced to cling to the edge. Whatever you can do to be kind to yourself will lower your stress and remind others of your importance.

2.
Life Isn't Fair—Get Over It

The fact that life isn't fair is often a hard truth to swallow (a little goat's milk or oily sardine treat helps). Yet sooner or later we each look in the mirror and face the same sobering truths: We are cats. We kick ass. Embrace the idea of yourself as infinitely superior to others. Only when you accept this universal truth can you help others come to grips with it.

3.
*Purr*spective:
Will This Matter a Year from Now?

Too often we allow ourselves to become entangled in "bad kitty" guilt. To combat negative self-meows, stop and ask yourself, "Will this matter a year from now?" For example, say you can't quite make it to your favorite spot on the living room carpet and instead toss your cookies (or kibbles) atop the new white bed-spread. Chances are that a year from now it will be a shredded, cat-hair-covered rag anyway, so is there really any harm in your action? No. Let it go and move on.

4.
Every Day, Tell at Least One Person Something You Like, Admire, or Appreciate about Him or Her

Finding and acknowledging the good in others quickly leads to finding and recognizing the good in ourselves. Offer a compliment that comes from the heart and bask in the glow of gratitude reflected back at you. Here are some sample compliments to help you get started:

- "I appreciate how I only have to walk on your face for a short time each morning before you get up to feed me."

- "Your sweater looks stunning with thousands of pulled threads hanging from it."

- "I admire your willingness to pick up my poo. I could never lower myself to do something like that."

Don't worry that you'll embarrass others with your generosity of spirit. More often than not, your compliments will bring tears to their eyes.

5.
Stop Pointing the Paw of Blame

Stop pointing the paw of blame—at yourself. As a rule, *always* blame others for things that go wrong. What purpose is served by your getting in trouble? Being exiled to the garage is no way to live. So you flung the African violets across the room. (Not your fault. The African violets started it.) To avoid being hassled about the mess, smear peanut butter on an African violet leaf, call the dog into the room, and let nature take its course. Then give yourself a pat on the back for contributing to his personal growth. After all, what is life without lessons learned from challenges?

6.
Stare into Strangers' Eyes and Smile (Unblinking, until You Break Them)

Confident cats don't dash under the bed when the doorbell rings or strange footsteps are heard in the hall. Instead, they weave their way into the room to demand more than their share of the attention. To welcome new friends (about whom you could care less), plant yourself directly in front of them, catch their gaze, and stare unblinking until they either break eye contact, shift uncomfortably, or start crying. At that point, rub your face against their legs, thereby declaring them and all their kin to be your eternal property.

7.
Become an Early Riser— and Force Others to Join You

The best way to greet the day is to get up early and take a moment to meditate, watch the sun rise, and reflect on the many ways you bless others with your presence. Treat mornings as "me" time, before the hustle and bustle of jingle ball chasing, bird gazing, and sunbeam lounging begins. A 3 or 4 a.m. wake-up plan is not unreasonable. Of course, you can't be expected to greet the day without fresh food and water, so make it part of your morning routine to stomp on the bladders of those you love until they haul themselves out of bed to give you the nourishment you require. They might be tempted to return to bed, but you can remedy this by curling up in the warm spot they left behind. No reason you can't do your morning meditation from there. They'll thank you for the jump-start you've given their day.

8.
Write Down Your Five Most Rigid Beliefs and See if You Can Soften Them

"All dogs are stupid." "The vacuum cleaner sucks." "Squirrels are nuts." "The sound of a tuna can being opened is pure Mozart." "Catnip is not addictive, and I only use it for medicinal purposes, anyway."

We all claw through life with preconceived notions. But examining and even rethinking long-held beliefs is a sign of enlightenment. So try rewording "All dogs are stupid" to "*Most* dogs are *probably* stupid," thereby leaving open the teeny-tiny possibility that maybe, someday, on a long shot, you'll meet one that isn't a complete idiot. Likewise, reframe "All screen doors are for climbing" to—well, okay, that one's pretty much set in stone. But you get the idea.

9.
Go Green

Can you even believe how many empty toilet paper rolls are just *thrown out*? Have humans no sense of imagination or wonder? To help humans recognize the value of the earth, scatter garbage around the yard and demonstrate, for example, how a simple paper bag becomes a fort, a cloaking device, or a place to hide the dog's favorite bone.

10.
Nurture a Plant

Pick a plant and love it unconditionally. Visit and rub against
it daily. Water it using whatever methods are available to you.
Dig in its soil as you would in the litter box to find the perfect
spot. Although you may be tempted, do not eat the—HEY. DO
NOT EAT THE PLANT. SPIT IT OUT, NOW. The plant
represents a journey toward inner peace and—I SEE THAT.
YOU KNOCKED THAT OVER ON PURPOSE, DIDN'T
YOU?—toward inner peace and—HEY! DROP IT. WE DO
NOT GNAW THE THINGS WE LOVE. You know what?
Forget the plant. Find yourself a nice squeaky toy and nurture
that instead.

11.
Refuse to Act Fetching

Fetch is an ancient Greek word meaning "to look stupid running
after something as if it's alive—and then turning around and
going all the way back." Cats do not speak Greek and therefore
the word is not in a cat's repertoire. Yet this doesn't stop humans
from winging jingle balls down the hall or waving cotton catnip
mice in our face. Remember that you don't have to do anything
you don't want to do. Relax. Go limp. Look the other way and
refuse to acknowledge the feeble attempts of others to engage
you. Fetch? Please. That toy mouse isn't going anywhere.

12.

Mind Your Own Business
(Unless Something Is Moved,
Changed, or Altered in
Any Way, in Which Case,
Investigate Immediately)

It's hard for a cat to mind his or her own business, simply because everything in life *is* your business. That's why you monitor the house, yard, kitchen countertops, and mesh screen on the fish tank for even the smallest of changes. Don't shy away from climbing into sinks, exploring bedsprings, and doing reconnaissance work from atop the fridge to stay abreast of breaking news. Houseguests require special monitoring because they can introduce unwanted change. You'll need to do some undercover work and explore every inch of their suitcases, preferably while all their clothes are still packed inside. Once you have crawled over, sniffed, licked, batted, clawed, and triumphed over whatever object has been brought in or moved, you may return to minding your own business from a disdainful distance.

13.
Give Up on the Idea That
More Is Better

Embrace the idea that more is *best!* More kibbles! More toys! More poop in the sandbox! The more stuff you have, the happier you'll be. Late night infomercials don't lie. Just because you have a room full of untouched cat toys doesn't mean you should be denied the latest scratch-and-sniff toy that emits mouselike squeaks when you carry it from room to room. He who dies with the most PetSmart playthings wins, and you are *not* going to let that stupid Siamese down the street out-bling you. Hoard everything and hope it's possible to bribe your way into Kitty Heaven.

14.
Repeat to Yourself,
"Life Isn't an Emergency"

Actually, all cats seem to have this one down. Carry on.

15.
When in Doubt, Chase Something

If you're feeling anxious or troubled, locate a fixed object in space, such as a shoelace, the dog, or a dust mite, and go on a rampage. Stalk it, pounce on it, and—if it dares put up a fight—chase it down the hall and smite it.

16.
Practice Being in the Eye of the Storm

The eye of the storm is the calm center in the middle of a hurricane or tornado. Ideally, you want to be the calm spot in the center of chaos. Of course, that means you must first stir up some chaos. Try tipping over a vase, pouncing out from under an ottoman to attack the dog, or altering the trajectory of the planet by racing in circles in the opposite direction of the earth's spin. Once you've established chaos, race to your favorite sun spot, throw yourself down, and go Zen. Raise a weary, sleep-filled eye when your human approaches and questions you about your whereabouts when the Christmas tree tipped over. "Huh? What are you talking about? I've been here all day."

17.
Be Willing to Learn from
Friends, Family, and Felines

All of the beings in your life exist because they have something to teach you. Observe the house parakeet, for example, chirping a joyful song in her cage. From her you can learn bravery and holding a positive attitude in the face of impending consumption. (It's just a matter of time before you figure out how to bridge the distance between the china cabinet and that cage.) The dog knows how to nudge open the cabinet where the Milk-Bones are kept. Learn from him even though he's not smart enough to wait until no one is looking. Life is about keeping an open mind—or at least an open claw.

18.
Insist on Befriending
Those Who Hate Cats

If your "anti-cat" radar goes off and tells you a cat hater is in range, race immediately to the person in distress, jump in his or her lap, and release copious amounts of fur on the person's clothes (the theory being that, once these people look like you, they'll have to love you). You may also attempt to knead such a person into submission. If he or she pushes you aside, perch like a vulture on the arm of the person's chair and stare at the his or her neck. Your charms are impossible to resist. Soon you'll wear down the person's defenses and he or she will be putty in your paws.

19.
Leave Your Mark on the World

Scent mark *everything*. Couches, door frames, pillows, appliances, houseguests—claim everything as yours. Be wary of sharing. Once you allow humans on the bed or couch once or twice, their smell gets on it and they're going to think they belong there.

20.
Make Peace with Human Imperfection

Face it: Humans are fallible. You are engaging in self-defeating behaviors if you attempt to hold them up to feline standards. You've seen them in the morning before their first cup of coffee— there's only so much raw material there to work with. Love them for the sweet, well-meaning, clueless creatures they are, and they'll do just about anything for you in return.

CHAPTER SIX

Nice Cats Don't Get the Corner Litter Box

We're not sure why humans are determined to spend hours creating minutes in a place called "the bored room," although the PowerPoint laser light, the fact that dogs eat dogs, and the ongoing rumors of a rat race do add a hint of intrigue. In order to see what people do with their day (and to prove the hypothesis that the answer is "not much"), cats across the nation are invading cor*purr*ate America, sleeping on delete keys, jamming printers with executive-ego-sized hairballs, and shredding any memo that displeases them.

Cats have a head for business, whether it's their own or a spare one they bring in from a ratty competitor and drop at the smokers' entrance. They also enjoy being involved in other people's business. This makes them ideal cor*purr*ate spies, human resource personnel, and middle managers, who not only look over employees' shoulders as they work, but actually perch on those shoulders for hours on end to ensure that the work gets done.

If you're a cat who wants to attack the competition as if it's a chipmunk covered in catnip, you'll need to refine your feline wiles and let people know you mean business. In other words, never let them see your whiskers twitch. Use the checklist below to determine what areas in your CEO (Cats Expecting Obedience) repertoire might need reinforcing. Lick all that apply.

_____ I'm often described as "manipulative," "bossy," or "pure evil."

_____ Unless a water pistol is involved, I rarely back down.

_____ I don't hesitate to go over someone's head (especially around 3 a.m. while he or she is sleeping).

_____ The only open-door policy I have is that every door remains open to *me*.

_____ I am known for aggressively asserting my opinion and being willing to claw, throw up near, or nap on anyone who disagrees with me.

_____ You need only look at me to realize that, frankly, my dear, I don't give a damn.

_____ I prefer to think "inside the box," especially cardboard packing boxes or even grocery bags—although an empty drawer in the employee kitchen will do in a pinch.

_____ I have strong international negotiation skills. English bulldogs, Japanese fighting fish, and Siberian dwarf hamsters cave before me.

_____ "Compromise" isn't in my vocabulary.

_____ I see most employees as chew toys—no, wait—as valuable resources. Ha-ha, just kidding—I see them as chew toys.

If you looked at this checklist and immediately squatted and defecated on it and then called your poodle intern in to clean up the mess, congratulations—you are not a nice cat and there's nothing more we can teach you. If you actually filled out the checklist, then you've got a lot to learn. Keep reading.

It's time to stop living a life defined by the needs of others. Just think of what is asked of you on a daily basis: leave the printer alone, don't shed on my suit, spit out that eraser, get off my head, and on and on.

As nice cats, we too often kill ourselves (wasting a perfectly good life or two) trying to please others and live by rules not suited to a cat's lifestyle, temperament, or strict beauty regime. No more. Shake off the chains of domesticity and return to your innate "I will stalk and eat you and this entire village if I have to" roots. Starting today, it's time to remind everyone who the big chief is.

Self-Assessment

Use the scale below to rate your exe*cat*ive behaviors. Be honest. Remember, all you have to do is purr and people will promote you.

1 = Rarely true, 2 = Sometimes true, 3 = Almost always true

1. Rules are for pussycats. _____

2. I can make anyone pet me—if I feel like it. _____

3. I'm realistic about how much I can accomplish in any one day with the twenty to thirty minutes I'm awake. _____

4. I am valued for my contributions to the bottom line—mostly because I can lick it. _____

5. I'm not afraid to turn "psycho cat" when the situation warrants it. _____

6. I'm willing to accept blame, except that nothing is ever my fault. _____

7. I can hold a grudge longer than I can hold a dead mouse in my mouth. _____

8. I am good at calling attention to myself—like this: mrow-mrow-mrow-mrow-mrow-mrow-mrow-mrow-mrow. _____

9. It's better to beg for forgiveness than to ask for permission. _____

10. Asking for permission *and* begging for forgiveness is for wimps. _____

11. I can dominate any conference table by casually walking across everyone's paperwork as if I don't know what I'm doing. _____

12. Briefcases are for sleeping in (or for emergency visits when the executive washrooms are being cleaned). _____

13. If I don't like what someone is saying, I leave the room while he or she is still talking. _____

14. If I perceive others as wasting my time, I throw myself at their feet and feign death. _____

15. I steal others' ideas, and anything else they are foolish enough to leave lying around. _____

16. I drive a hard bargain and can outstare anyone, unless I hear a can opener. _____

17. I consciously spend time each day engaged in—zzzzzzzzz—huhza? What? _____

18. *Face time* is best defined as the amount of time I spend waving my tail in someone's face. _____

19. If I inadvertently offend someone, I don't worry about it. It probably won't greatly affect *my* life. _____

20. I'm not afraid to ask for a raise—or for a hand in getting down from the indoor cat tree. _____

21. My personal grooming habits are impeccable. _____

22. *Circling back* refers to my path around the employees' legs. _____

23. Employee raises should be based on who smells the most like tuna. _____

24. I fire those who question my sanity when I occasionally run up and down the hall like my tail is on fire. (Holy crap, it's not, is it?) _____

25. My belly is not to be touched. Like a cigarette behind glass, it's there to tempt you but only to be reached for in an emergency. _____

SCORING

Have you learned nothing? What did we *just* tell you about taking quizzes? Bad kitty! Still, if you caved and took the test, here are your results:

25 points: Horrible, horrible, horrible. Are you spending all your time with dogs? Start acting like a cat or we'll send the kitty mafia in the form of a sphynx named Rocko "The Claw" Mouser to deal with you.

26 to 39: You call yourself a threat? People are laughing at you, and not just because you're so cute when you pounce on your jingle ball.

40 to 50: You suffer from a classic case of oversocialization. The life of a pampered cat is a good one, as long as you still show them the tiger in you now and again. Cats were once worshipped as gods. Demand that we as a society return to this standard.

51 to 64: You have your moments—perhaps an unexpected pounce or a swift claw to the ankle—but you need more *cat*titude. The spirit of a bold cat is in there, waiting to be released. A little fine-tuning and a snort of catnip in the cor*purr*ate bathroom for confidence, and you'll be on your way.

65 to 75: Paws up! You are one badass kitty! Confident, assertive, and manipulative (but still a looker), you are the cat people are desperate to rub up against. You're used to getting your way and refuse to compromise on your principles. Congratulations on having clawed your way to the top.

The Difference Between Cats and Dogs in the Workplace

There's a reason the nouns in the phrases *catnap* and *work like a dog* aren't interchangeable. For those foolish enough to follow the canine instincts of fidelity, trust, and honor—good luck to you. For the rest of us, who will actually be *running* the world, here's a little primer on why cat shenanigans will always trump a strong work ethic.

DOG: Do as you're told without question and for little to no pay.
CAT: Blink slowly at any request, then sashay down the hall without replying, swishing your tail and leaving people to wonder if you heard them.

DOG: A positive attitude goes a long way. Greet everyone with an eager tail wag and a lick of appreciation.
CAT: Draw blood from those who dare to question your authority.

DOG: When the boss keeps you waiting over an hour for your scheduled appointment, take it in stride and greet him as if you haven't seen him for a year.
CAT: If someone leaves the room, even momentarily, stare at the person warily when he or she returns as if you've never seen the person before in your life. Then call secu-

rity to report a trespasser on the premises and have him
or her escorted out.

DOG: I hope my coworkers like me.
CAT: Others work here? Excellent. Have one of them fetch
me a rodent, stat.

DOG: The people are the heart and soul of our company.
CAT: I appreciate the many minions loitering in the hall.
It makes it that much easier to climb the cor*purr*ate ladder
when I can use their heads and backs as a launching pad
for my meteoric rise.

DOG: What, quitting time already? Oh, no! I can't make
it until tomorrow without seeing you! Do you want to
do something together tonight? Do you? Do you?
CAT: Wake me up at 4:59 p.m. so I can get out of this
hellhole on time, will you?

DOG: What? Me? A promotion? This is so unexpected!
Thank you for your confidence in me! I won't disappoint
you! I'd work here for free, you know.
CAT: I just crowned myself king. Your new title is "Num-
Nums," and I want you to hum "Mr. Mistoffelees" nonstop
for a week or you're fired.

Nine Unconscious Mistakes Cats Make, and How to Fix Them Without Anyone Ever Knowing

If your score from the self-assessment quiz shows a less-than-ideal knack for cor*purr*ate takeovers, it's time to restrategize. Take a look around: Are you getting your fair share? Who has the biggest office? Who controls the distribution of treats and canned food? Why does accounting refuse to list the mouse you dragged in among company assets? (Suddenly people are concerned with cor*purr*ate ethics?)

If you're not the one in charge, something is horribly wrong. Below are the top nine mistakes made by cats in the workplace, along with practical suggestions to modify nonfeline behaviors.

MISTAKE #1: DOING ANYTHING THAT EVEN REMOTELY RESEMBLES WORK

Dogs work. Cats shirk. Your one and only role in the workforce is to determine what needs to be accomplished and then avoid it at all costs.

Suggestions:

• Engage in MBSA—Management by Stalking Around. Constant circling makes you hard to track down. However, if the person attempting to assign you work appears to be pulling closer, don't hesitate to run.

- If caught catnapping, explain that you're in the middle of a 360-degree evaluation. Rotate your body in a full circle, lie back down, and return to sleep.

- Carry a newspaper and, when stopped, explain that you're on the way to the litter box to leave a stinky. People will give you a wide berth.

MISTAKE #2: ACCEPTING FEEDBACK

You are a cat. You do not—ever—accept critiques from someone else (as if anyone is qualified to judge you anyway).

Suggestions:

- Only pretend you're interested in self-development. Act as if you are jotting down others' suggestions on sticky notes, but instead write, "I am better than you," and stick it to their computers.

- Avoid goal setting. There are better ways to spend your time than in self-evaluation.

- Sleeping under the desk comes to mind.

MISTAKE #3: OFFERING A LIMP PAWSHAKE

Aha! Trick question. Cats should *never* offer to shake paws, fetch, or perform any other "trick" that would have others seeing you as the trained office seal or—God forbid—dog.

Suggestions:

- If someone offers you food in exchange for sitting, speaking, or any other behavior, stare up at him or her quizzically, as if your native language is ancient Latin. Then grab the food and run.

- If it's unavoidable that you "shake" with someone, extend those claws and dig in. First one to let go or pass out loses.

MISTAKE #4: QUID PRO QUO

Commonly known as "You scratch my back, and I'll scratch yours," quid pro quo is something to be avoided in the life of a cat. The more standard feline rule is "You scratch my back, and when that ends, we're done here."

Suggestions:

- A better rule to remind people of when dealing with cats is caveat emptor, or "Let the scratcher beware." Remember, even when you've got a contract in writing, if you can shred it they can't prove it existed.

- If you are tricked into signing a contract that obligates you to do anything, spray it. Cat urine is recognized in most courts of law as a universal invalidator of any agreement.

MISTAKE #5: NEEDING TO BE LIKED

Having a desire to be liked is a more common mistake among cats than one might suspect. There's nothing wrong with being a soft touch on the inside. You just need to be careful, otherwise people will come to expect your unconditional love and devotion. Then—obviously—you're screwed.

Suggestions:

- Identify your fear. Is it not knowing where the next ear scratch might come from? Are you nervous that the mouse you left in the executives' fridge will be discovered? Channel those fears into positive actions, such as faxing a copy of your butt to the accounting department or leaping off the top of a filing cabinet to frighten the temp. Your fears will soon vanish.

- Remember, *you* like you. Head over to the mirror for some "me time," and you'll see what we mean.

MISTAKE #6: NEGOTIATING DURING DAYLIGHT HOURS

Negotiations (such as "Am I allowed to eat the office plants, how often, and how much?") are all about timing, so *when* you approach the boss with a question is key. We suggest between the hours of midnight and 4 a.m., because this is when humans are most receptive. The typical human response at this time ranges from "Do whatever you want. Just shut up and leave me alone" to "Mmuumph," which may be interpreted in any number of ways. You may now eat the plants, relocate your litter box to the cubicle of that annoying guy next to you, and push your own pet project ahead of everyone else's, all thanks to your stellar bargaining skills.

Suggestions:

- Keep a straight face during negotiations. You know you're going to win, but it's considered bad manners to laugh in the boss's face.

- Forget the midnight talks and just do whatever you want, whenever you feel like it. It's going to amount to the same outcome.

- Go ahead and laugh. What are they going to do? Fire you?

MISTAKE #7: ALLOWING YOURSELF TO BE BULLIED

It's a cat's duty to go limp atop the annual report during an executive retreat. It's a subtle hint that maybe the staff should work on making the report a little more *interesting* next year. Yet people seem to take offense. If you've ever allowed yourself to be shooed off a report, laptop, or the table where a catered in-house luncheon is being served, then you need some intervention.

Suggestions:

- If a human insists on shooing you off something, like the desk or a shoulder, wait thirty seconds and hop back up. Repeat as necessary. Sooner or later the person will question whether chasing you away is worth the effort.

- Practice role reversal. Shoo any person off a chair, couch, or floor space that's to your liking. Even if he or she isn't bothering you by being in that spot, it's still good to establish an early dominance.

MISTAKE #8: IGNORING OFFICE POLITICS

Like a flea dip after a romp in the woods, office politics are unavoidable. It's to your advantage to stay in the know. If you don't pay attention to who's feuding with whom, how will you be able to stir up mischief?

Suggestions:

- Network. Break kibble with fellow cats, stay on speaking terms with the postman, and be kind to the fish (until you figure out a way to penetrate what will one day become their watery grave). Even an occasional lunch with the dog may yield information you can put to good use. Plus, that gives you the chance to steal his lunch.

- Keep an ear close to the ground. The easiest way to do this is to nap on the floor, but whatever works.

- Maintain relations with local cats, including the ferals that hang out by the dumpster on Main. You never know when a little "muscle" might come in handy.

MISTAKE #9: STAYING IN YOUR SAFETY ZONE (OTHERWISE KNOWN AS "BED")

Like our human counterparts, cats are creatures of habit. That's why you'll find yourself bouncing up and down on your coworker's bed in the wee hours, eager for a little attention—it's what you've always done, so why change? Yet catching coworkers off guard has its advantages. Keep the humans guessing by occasionally leaving your comfort zone.

Suggestions:

- Set the alarm and haul yourself out of bed at some ungodly hour like noon to take stock of what's happening around you.

- Every few weeks, move to a new spot in the office and claim it as your new napping area. The break room, in front of the receptionist area, and under the CEO's desk are all spots worth considering.

Are You a Career Cat or Stay-at-Home Mouser?

Now that you know *how* to survive cor*purr*ate America, you need to decide if you even care to be there. You may wish to join cats across the nation as they invade offices, plant their feather wands atop polished wood tables, give their private parts a few celebratory licks, and then call it a day. Or you may find your bliss (that's "bliss, not "hiss") on the home front, making homemade mouse pies and napping on laundry pulled hot from the dryer. Whichever your choice, the tests below can match your interests and personality to see if prowling the cor*purr*ate world is right for you.

CIRCLE UP TO TEN WORDS THAT BEST DESCRIBE YOUR PERSONALITY:

Agile	Calm	Daunting
Anal Retentive	Cheerful	Dictatorial
Approachable	Clingy	Domineering
Assertive	Clownish	Doubting
Authoritative	Clumsy	Fearless
Balanced	Confused	Flexible
Bloated	Cunning	Fun
Boisterous	Curious	Furtive
Bored	Cute	Fussy

Glowing	Manic	Respectful
Greedy	Meticulous	Sassy
Gregarious	Moody	Sluggish
Hissy	Optimistic	Snarky
Hungry	Passive	Soft
Innocent	Patient	Strong
Intense	*Purr*fect	Sweet
Introspective	*Purr*suasive	Territorial
Lazy	Pessimistic	Tricky
Limp	Prissy	Warped
Lithe	Purring	Water Averse

CIRCLE FIVE WORDS YOU THINK OTHERS MOST USE TO DESCRIBE YOU:

Astonishing	Kingly	*Purr*fect
Awe Inspiring	Majestic	*Purr*fect
Brave	Mensa-ish	*Purr*fect
Breathtaking	Mystical	*Purr*fect
Godlike	Omnipotent	Queenly
Incredible	Priceless	Striking
Kick-Ass	*Purr*fect	Stunning

LIST YOUR TOP FIVE TRANSFERABLE SKILLS.

For example:

1. Rolling in dirt

2. Gaining entry to impossible places (air-conditioning ducts, the snack cabinet, Harvard)

3. Ability to hear a can opener from two miles away

4. Leaping over tall buildings, houseplants, coffee tables, and stationary dogs in a single bound

5. An alertness that verges on paranoia

NOW LIST THREE WAYS YOU ENJOY SPENDING YOUR TIME.

For example:

1. Napping

2. Napping upside down

3. Postnap napping

WHAT ARE YOUR TOP THREE STRENGTHS?

For example:

1. Beauty

2. Hygiene

3. Balancing on ledges, mantels, and full bladders

WHAT ARE YOUR TOP THREE WEAKNESSES?

For example:

1. Excessive shedding when under duress

2. Lack of follow-through (e.g., mouse, half dead)

3. Tendency to show others my backside when I'm angry, annoyed, or frustrated, or on days ending in *y*

Now that you know a little bit more about yourself, take those skills and insert them into a resume. We've attached a sample one on the following page. Feel free to be a copycat.

Bottom line? (No, not *your* bottom line. Look up. Here. Don't clean your butt. Look here. At *me*.) Being nice gets you nowhere. The cor*purr*ate world is just waiting for you to pounce. Don't disappoint them.

K.T. KACHT

555 Paws Way • Allabout, ME 11111 • ktkacht@aol-rowr.com

OBJECTIVE

Often aloof and reserved but sometimes wildly enthusiastic individual seeks a high-level (top of the refrigerator or higher) supervisory position to build on people skills and showcase ability to focus on small, moving dots of light. Self-motivator with strong desire to advance . . . slowly . . . and stealthily.

OVERVIEW

- Experienced rodent headhunter with four years' and two lives' experience
- Ability to react quickly—and unexpectedly—to others
- Background in small animal intestine removal
- Able to attack the hand at task
- Responsible for rodent RIF (reduction in force) in an underperforming barn by more than 30 percent in a twelve-month time period
- Special expertise in voles, garden snakes, and wheatgrass
- Proven record of accomplishment in Management by Stalking Around (MBSA)
- Instituted and enforced a corporate-wide open-pet-door policy

CORE COMPETENCIES

- Not afraid to question or ignore authority—repeatedly
- Will eat frogs and grass
- Strong attention to detail (especially if it flinches or attempts to flee)
- Comprehensive knowledge of sleep deprivation tactics
- Healthy curiosity about the way things work
- Ability to vomit on demand
- Excel at sleep-life balance
- Well-groomed
- Team player—in teams of one
- Excellent negotiator who refuses to take "No" or "Stop or I will ship you to Greenland" for an answer

- Strong networker with ability to feign interest in what others have to say
- Demonstrated ability to always land on feet; also pretty good on a narrow ledge

JOB EXPERIENCE
Rodent Headhunter August 2007 – Present
- Decapitated wide array of "clients" over two-year period
- Sponsored corporate "give back" programs that resulted in one-third higher back porch contributions
- Located and developed highest-quality sunbeam spots
- Invented the patented "Cooperate and I Might Let You Live" negotiation system

Night Security Guard February 2005 – July 2007
- Patrolled assigned areas on foot, including closets, storage areas, crawl spaces, and interior walls
- Implemented whisker detection system
- Provided escort services for crickets, flies, stray leaves, and dead bugs
- Scaled doors, windows, screens, and baby gates to uncover security gaps
- Informed violators of rule infractions, such as loitering, smoking, or showing affection to dogs
- Monitored mouse and bird population
- Performed periodic checks of litter overflow system
- Sounded alarm when presence of unauthorized persons, or a shadow, detected

Stay-at-Home Mouser 2003 – 2004

COMPUTER SKILLS
PawerPoint skills; MS-DOZE platform; strong Internet skills involving keyboard napping applications; proficient with mouse

HOBBIES
Yoga, short-distance sprinting, competitive napping, raw food movement volunteer

References Available upon Request (but I will kill you)

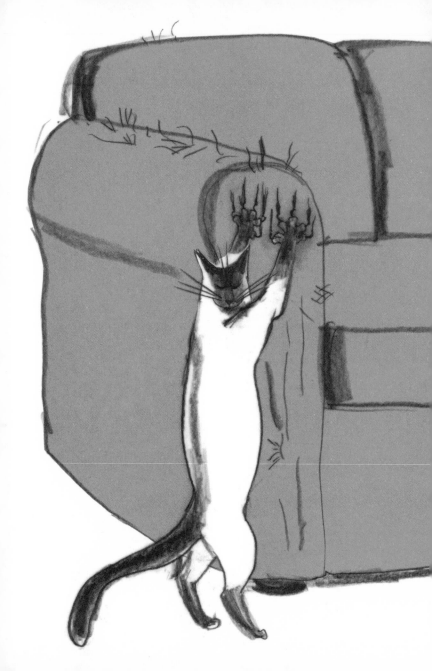

CHAPTER SEVEN

The 7 Habits of Highly Effective Cats

Every moment in a cat's life offers choices. Will you brave a perilous exploration of the dusty reaches of the game closet or stick with the familiarity of the embroidered pillow on the couch? Slink away from the crime scene formerly known as "the hall rug" or face the music? Teach a daddy longlegs who his daddy really is or allow him to crawl off with what's left of his dignity? Claw the sofa like a harp or use Mom's new pantyhose instead?

Remember, for you to win, someone else needs to lose. Win-win scenarios are for weak-minded creatures or species without retractable claws. We've pieced together seven principles every cat should adhere to in order to live the best possible life.* Adopt these seven habits and take your hair-raising antics to a whole new level.

* There would have been nine principles, but we were distracted by a moving red dot of light.

Habit #1:
Agree to Disagree

Humans will sometimes be less than enthused about your natural exuberance for life. It may be necessary for you to agree to disagree with them on whether, for example, the potted plants in the house exist solely for your amusement. But why else would God create shih tzus, bubble wrap, and Boston ferns except to keep you entertained?

Habit #2:
Claim Everything as Yours

The minute you enter a room, quickly mark everything there as yours. We prefer a label gun, but you can go old-school and rub your scent on anything that stands still. Even if you're not particularly interested in an item, such as a scratching post (hello—it's not like we don't already have a sofa), it's best to mark it as belonging to you. That way there are fewer legal questions when you auction the items off on eBay.

Habit #3:
Always Keep a Clean Butt

Well . . . *yeah*.

Habit #4:
Jump on It Before It Jumps on You

A cat's life revolves around being ever vigilant. Let your guard down for one minute and you may find a kitty porn video of you licking certain private places being circulated on YouTube. Attack first and ask questions later. Assume that everyone and everything—shadows, twist ties, your tail—is out to get you.

Habit #5:
When in Doubt, Sleep It Out

Who are we? Why are we here? Where are you going with that ham? Questions such as these have plagued introspective felines since the beginning of time. But until the answers reveal themselves, a little catnap never hurt to clear the mind.

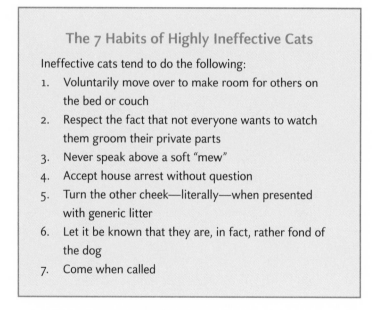

The 7 Habits of Highly Ineffective Cats

Ineffective cats tend to do the following:

1. Voluntarily move over to make room for others on the bed or couch
2. Respect the fact that not everyone wants to watch them groom their private parts
3. Never speak above a soft "mew"
4. Accept house arrest without question
5. Turn the other cheek—literally—when presented with generic litter
6. Let it be known that they are, in fact, rather fond of the dog
7. Come when called

Habit #6:
Act Completely Different at the Vet's Office than You Do at Home

There are few things more fun in life than watching your human explain to a mauled and bleeding vet tech that you *never* act like this at home! Bonus points if you manage to leap off the exam table at any time during your physical.

Habit #7:
Create a Sense of Lingering Inferiority in Humans

It's never too early or too late to mock your human for his or her flaws and minor im*purr*fections. Do your job right, and you can turn a small concern about a bulbous nose or a lackluster career into a full-blown fetish—the outcome being hours of attention paid to you as your human seeks solace and comfort in your presence. (You've gotta love the irony.)

Personal Mission Statement (PMS) for Cats

While the 7 Habits of Highly Effective Cats will help you handle most of what life throws at you, self-aware felines will also wish to fashion a personal mission statement. The statement is something you can return to time and again to remind yourself of your core values. A Cat's Personal Mission Statement (Cat PMS) will clarify the following:

- Who you are

- What you want

- What level of aggression is necessary to achieve your goals

Here are a few sample Cat PMSs:

My name is Emma. I want to go outside. I am willing to lie hidden for hours behind the sofa in the hopes that an all-out dash for the front door when it opens will gain me my freedom. Cats rule, dogs drool!

My name is Mr. Snicker-Bottoms. I want free-range grazing rights to the kibble bag and to abolish the "no cats allowed on the countertops" rule. I am willing to maintain a picket line outside the kitchen day and night for my beliefs. I believe that consistently applying sleep-deprivation tactics to my humans will see me through to victory. I like squeaky toys. I would not be averse to a name change.

I am Fluffy, the Orange Blur! A master of disguise, I see you, but you do not see me. I am the glittering eyes under the stairs, the sudden movement you almost glimpse from the corner of your eye. My goal is nothing less than world domination. I believe that if I slink around corners long enough, my genius will be recognized and humans will fall in line, probably because they will trip over me. I will rule my evil empire forever! (Barring world domination, I would like a new jingle ball.)

Ready to create your own PMS? We've given you some ideas to start with, but you can just fill in the blanks as you see fit.

My name is _____.

More than anything else in life, I want _____.

- My reproductive parts back
- Ham
- Outside/inside
- To take the dog for a "walk"
- Wii Bowling
- A car, a squirrel, a road, thirty seconds, and *no questions asked*

I am willing to _____ *to get what I want.*

- Allow my belly to be touched. Briefly. Wait! I changed my mind. No deal.
- Resort to terrorist actions.
- Unleash the hounds!
- Release toxic kitty gas.
- Stomp on your face.
- I'm not changing anything about myself. Period.

The 7 Habits of Highly Effective Cat "Owners":

Effective cat "owners" tend to have the following characteristics:

1. Come when called
2. Always smell like tuna
3. Be immune to electrostatic shock
4. Be telepathic, so there's no need for you to actually leave your sunspot to tell them you've got a small itch behind your left ear that needs tending to
5. Be willing to ditch the boyfriend/girlfriend/spouse/ asthmatic child who doesn't like or can't tolerate cats
6. Acknowledge that sleeping placements on the bed are settled on a first-come, first-served basis
7. Have warm hands, warm feet, and a warm heart

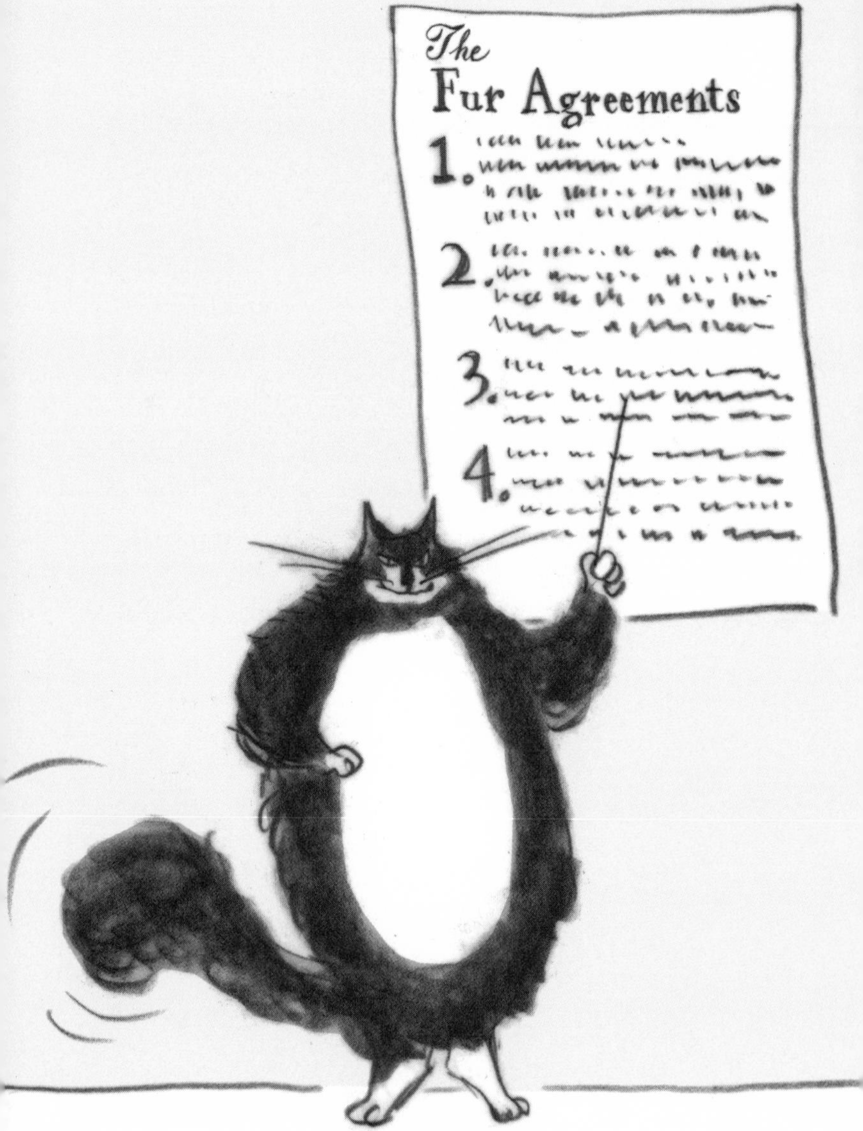
The
Fur Agreements
1.
2.
3.
4.

CHAPTER EIGHT

The Fur Agreements

Based on ancient—from before the invention of multicat litter—wisdom, the Four Agreements are principles set forth by healer Don Miguel Ruiz to raise the spiritual vibrations of humans in the hopes that they'll finally get it together and stop watching so much *American Idol*.

However, humans haven't quite figured out how to implement these spiritual principles in their daily lives. Therefore, it's up to today's cats to hold humans accountable to live principled lives. Naturally, the feline approach to these principles is a little different from the human approach. Below is a comparison of the agreements set out by Ruiz and our newly improved and updated version for felines.

THE FOUR AGREEMENTS	THE FUR AGREEMENTS
Be Impeccable with Your Word	Hold Others to Their Word
Don't Take Anything Personally	Don't Take Anything *Purr*sonally—Unless Holding a Grudge Works to Your Advantage
Don't Make Assumptions	Assume Everyone Else Is an Idiot (It Saves Time)
Always Do Your Best	Always Do Your Best—Unless You Can Get Away with Less

Fur Agreement #1:
Hold Others to Their Word

Suppose your person says, "I'll throw the jingle ball in just a minute." First of all, cats can't tell time, so thanks for that reminder. And second, how *dare* humans assume they have any choice in the matter of when the sacred jingle ball is to be thrown? If we want to chase the jingle ball, we want to chase it *now*.

Or, suppose, upon leaving the house, your humans tell you to have a good day, and then you don't. Whose fault is that? Surely not yours.

That's why it's important for us to hold humans to their word. If they tell us to have a good day, then, by God, they had better do something to ensure it happens.

HOW STRONG IS YOUR WORD?

While the average human's word is worth about as much as that hairball you coughed up this morning, a cat's word is to be trusted. If we say, "Mrow-pssft," we mean, "Mrow-pssft."

To inspire humans to follow your example, give your word often, in a loud, wailing tone of voice. You want to be sure everyone hears how impeccable you are being with your word. The word has the power to create. Give the word and watch humans race to fill your food dish. Give the word and watch the screen door slide open to allow you unfettered access to the outdoors. Give the word and watch your humans roll over, giving you the coveted center spot in bed. The word is magic in what it can create. Be mindful of its power and use it for good . . . or for evil. Whatever.

Fur Agreement #2:
Don't Take Anything *Purr*sonally— Unless Holding a Grudge Works to Your Advantage

Cats dig in the sandbox of low self-esteem whenever they look to humans to justify their existence. If someone utters an inane opinion such as "Bad kitty! Get out of the fish tank!" or "I used the can opener to open a can of peas, not tuna. Look—P-E-A-S," you must not take such statements to heart. In the above examples, you might turn a deaf ear and burp up a goldfish scale to show you won't be poisoned by negativity, or you might harass your human until he or she breaks down and opens a can of tuna just to be rid of you.

Although you are never to take anything *purr*sonally, you must ingrain in your humans the fact that your every tail flick and whisker twitch holds meaning, while leaving them completely clueless as to what that meaning may be. Like a high-level CIA operative or a fifteen-year-old-girl, you must never let others know exactly what you're thinking or what they may have done to upset you. What matters is that they now must spend time sucking up to you in the hopes of winning entry back in your good graces.

Remember, how many hugs or treats you're given per day should never influence your self-esteem. All you need concern yourself with is whether you have the capacity to make your humans halt all activity—such as making dinner or engaging in the act of procreation—and pay attention to you on demand.

Fur Agreement #3:
Assume Everyone Else Is an Idiot
(It Saves Time)

Cats sometimes make the mistake of giving people more credit than they're due. We like to believe people are capable of higher thought and emotion, a syndrome known as anthropomorphization (Latin for "wishful thinking"). We assume people experience fear, pain, anger, sadness, and happiness the way we do. In fact, most people lack the depth and range of emotions of even the most mentally deranged house cat. It's one of the reasons cats hang around humans. We're here to teach them the meaning of pure, unadulterated love—without the drool and mildewy smell that accompanies the same emotion in dogs.

How often has this happened to you? You're tucked into your favorite spot, perhaps an embroidered chair that receives direct sun, lulled to sleep by the warmth and silence of the home. Suddenly, a giant feather rustles in front of your face. You open one eye to take a peek and, having no interest, close it again. Now the feather is poked into your side and a voice from above sings, "Coochie-coochie coo! Get the feather! C'mon kitty-witty, get da big bad fe-der!"

Naturally, you assume that the voice has you confused with the family dog, who is willing to do everything short of eating turds (oh wait, he does that too) in order to please. Or you assume God is testing your patience. In fact, none of this is true. The reason for the feather in the face is—get this—that your person actually thinks you *like* it.

"*What?*" you say. "How can this be? I've made no indication that I want to chase the feather. Any moron can see that all I want to do is sleep."

That's the fascinating part. People think they're being kind when they thrash the bedraggled feather in our face. Ironically, many felines unintentionally encourage such behavior when, in an effort to rid themselves of the human and the feather, they reluctantly take a swipe or two at the object looming in front of them, thereby encouraging the behavior.

The way to avoid false assumptions is through clear and direct communication. Unlike cats, who are psychic (how else would we know to hide on the days we're scheduled to visit the

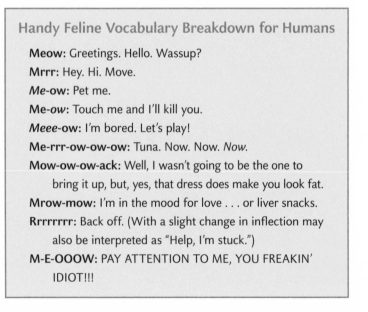

Handy Feline Vocabulary Breakdown for Humans

Meow: Greetings. Hello. Wassup?

Mrrr: Hey. Hi. Move.

***Me*-ow:** Pet me.

Me-*ow*: Touch me and I'll kill you.

***Meee*-ow:** I'm bored. Let's play!

Me-rrr-ow-ow-ow: Tuna. Now. Now. *Now.*

Mow-ow-ow-ack: Well, I wasn't going to be the one to bring it up, but, yes, that dress does make you look fat.

Mrow-mow: I'm in the mood for love . . . or liver snacks.

Rrrrrrr: Back off. (With a slight change in inflection may also be interpreted as "Help, I'm stuck.")

M-E-OOOW: PAY ATTENTION TO ME, YOU FREAKIN' IDIOT!!!

vet?), people need matters spelled out for them. Clip out the handy chart we've included and post it in a handy spot, such as near the toilet, where your person can review it often.

Fur Agreement #4: Always Do Your Best—Unless You Can Get Away with Less

Doing our best comes naturally to felines. Without even trying, we're always the best-looking creatures in any room, not to mention the smartest, most graceful and—it goes without saying— the most fashion forward.

Yet some days we're tired. Maybe we only got fifteen hours of sleep the day before. Maybe the motorized hamster ball is on our last nerve. Or maybe we've been hitting the catnip a little hard this week. Regardless, we start cutting corners. Perhaps we let the dog walk by without taking a swipe. Or maybe we poop outside the litter box because crawling inside is just too much effort. (This is not to be confused with pooping outside the litter box because we want the record to be clear on how we feel about our humans taking a long weekend and leaving us behind.)

You may accept the occasional "less than" from yourself, but refuse to accept it in others. You will find life flowing much more smoothly once you start *insisting* that your humans do their very best. Lapses you've previously allowed—an empty food dish, sharing the couch, your toys being picked up before you're done with them—will no longer be tolerated. Why? Because you *say so*, that's why.

Indeed, humans will suffer in the self-improvement department unless someone is there to point out each and every one of their personal flaws along the way. Luckily, they have you. How you point out areas that need attention will be a reflection of your *purr*sonality. Those with retiring *purr*sonalities might hide under the bed until a major faux pas, such as allowing another cat in the house, has been corrected. Those who aren't afraid to be more direct in their communication may feel free to jump in their human's lap, plant their paws on the person's chest, and have a little heart-to-heart.

Of course, the need to keep humans in line is something we can all be in agreement about.

CHAPTER NINE

A Cat's Worst-Case Scenario Survival Handbook

Are you ready to survive and thrive under the worst circumstances life throws at you? Would you last ten minutes outside the house with no access to the electric can opener *or* the lime green afghan on the couch? Get ready to find out!

Survival turns serious when you're faced with perils such as the cat carrier or a dinner served five minutes late. In this chapter you'll pick up tips on outwitting poisonous plants and refusing medication, and study how to subdue restless limbs lurking under the covers at night. Learn what to do in potentially awkward social situations (for example, when you discover something hanging from your butt), and how to disengage your favorite blankey from the wash without ever getting wet.

Scattered throughout the chapter are "Which Is Your Worst Case?" dilemmas to get you thinking about how you might handle your own life-and-death dramas. Get ready for action, because we're going to show you how to survive the *worst* that life has to dish out!

Which Is Your Worst Case...

Having a second cat in the house or global thermonuclear war?

How to Survive When Lost

Freedom isn't always all it's cracked up to be. If you find yourself outside, wandering unfamiliar territory, remember the following guidelines.

DO NOT PANIC
Unless it is near dinnertime and no food is in sight. Then, by all means, move into unrestrained terror.

STAY HIDDEN
It is not your job to find your humans. It is their job to find you. If this requires them to crawl on rooftops, peer into rain gutters, and slide on their belly in mud and leaves in the crawl spaces of every house in the neighborhood, calling your name while you remain mute and statuelike in the bushes, so be it. (In fact, if you remembered to bring a video camera, this would be priceless footage.)

GO VERTICAL
Climb as high as you can to get a view of your surroundings. From a rooftop or top tree limb, the unrecognizable transforms itself into the known. You're then left with the problem of getting down from the tree, but at least you're not lost anymore.

How to Break Into a Car

Carjacking is a skill all cats should master. You never know when you might need a sweet ride.

THE STOWAWAY METHOD

By far the easiest and most popular of all breaking and entering techniques, the stowaway method requires slipping unseen into luggage or a grocery bag carried into the car by a human, and then slipping out once inside the vehicle. Reveal your trickery quickly. In this case, the goal isn't to actually go anywhere, but rather to let your humans know how freaking brilliant and sneaky you are.

THE HITCHHIKER METHOD

Hop into the backseat or crawl under a tarp and hit the open road. Once you arrive at your final destination, allow the driver of the automobile to read your collar tag, ensuring an embarrassing visit from your humans after they drive the forty-five miles to claim you.

THE WARM ENGINE METHOD (NOT RECOMMENDED)

The warm engine method places you in the underside of an automobile, but the result of this breaking and entering can end badly. We advise avoiding *all* engines until our feline field researchers discover what it is that brings these lifeless metal hunks roaring to life.

How to Cope with a Favorite Blankey or Toy in the Wash

The secret to dealing with this worst-case scenario is to stay tough mentally. Use the following tips to talk yourself through it.

GIVE YOUR TOY A PEP TALK

Given how you feel about a bath or the occasional squirt of H_2O from a plastic water pistol, you can only imagine the torture your blankey is enduring. Stand outside the washing machine and meow loudly, to let Mr. Blankey know that help is on the way.

SHRED SOMETHING

Shredding a shawl or antique quilt that is a favorite of your humans will release stress and remind them how you feel about laundry day. Soon they'll get the idea and just learn to live with the filth.

What to Do if You Encounter a Snake

Snakes are our friends. (Ha-ha, not really. If you see one, stomp on it. Or, follow the suggestions below.)

INVOLVE THE DOG

See if you can get Fifi the Brainless Wonder involved. Not all snakes are poisonous, and you may enjoy "playing" with one, but first you need to know what you're dealing with. If Fifi lives, it's probably safe to stalk the snake. Enjoy!

CHALLENGE THE SNAKE TO A KUNG FU CONTEST

Use this as a subterfuge to keep the snake busy until your human arrives with the shovel.

Which Is Your Worst Case . . .

Nail clippers or pill shooter?

INVITE IT INSIDE
Invite the snake to make itself at home and watch the fun begin.

How to Survive Being Bathed

What's up with the human need to dunk everything they own—including the Persian cat—in warm, sudsy water? We cats have *forgotten* more about keeping clean then humans will ever know. Still, if you find yourself being swept off your feet and heading toward the kitchen sink, here are some tips on what to do.

STOP, DROP, AND CLAW
Think Wolverine from *X-Men* and unsheathe those bad boy claws. Hook them into anything you pass—a door frame, a banister, or the spongy inner thighs of the person carrying you.

KNOW THY ENEMY
Humans are told to keep calm, stay positive, and speak in soothing tones while giving kitty a bath. Your mission is to destroy your humans' peace of mind to the point where they're still popping Prozac for their nerves for up to two years after the initial bathing event.

Which Is Your Worst Case . . .

Being locked outside or trapped inside?

How to Tell if a Plant Is Poisonous

You can sniff it, rub on it, and dig up its roots, but the only sure-fire way to tell if a plant is poisonous is to take a nibble. If eating the plant makes you throw up, well, let's not jump to conclusions. In all fairness, you do throw up quite often.

How to Subdue a Human

Humans can turn on you at a moment's notice. This behavior is most noticeable at night when they roll and flail with no regard for the cat trying to catch a few z's at the foot of the bed. To corral a human, try the following techniques.

TOE NIPPING
A gentle bite on the tootsies reminds humans that they use the bed at your discretion. If they don't take the hint, feel free to pounce on a wayward foot and wrestle it into submission.

GO FOR THE PACKAGE
You male cats know what we mean.

What to Do if You're Caught with Something Hanging from Your Butt

People will take their cue from you. Carry on like nothing's wrong, then discreetly wipe your backside on your human's bedspread at your earliest convenience.

How to Avoid Being Struck by Lightning

When outside, always stand next to something higher than you. We suggest boosting the dog up on a crate and standing next to it.

How to Cross the Street

Although we recommend that cats stay inside or in the vicinity of their own yard, sometimes a street crossing becomes a necessity, such as when the nice lady with the bunny slippers up the block calls your name because she has special salmon snackies.

TRADITIONAL METHOD

To cross a street, crouch in the ready position. Once you see a car approach, rock back and forth indecisively. When the car is almost in front of you, dart forward. When you hear the sound of screeching metal and cursing, you'll know you're almost there. Continue walking, leisurely, across the street. Pause at the other side to give yourself a quick "all is well" tongue bath.

ALTERNATIVE METHOD

Meander to the center of the street. Fall gracefully to the ground and keep your ear pressed to the pavement to listen for approaching cars as you indulge in a quick nap. At the sound of a car (or

---

Which Is Your Worst Case . . .

Doll clothes or lion haircut?

---

the sound of your human yelling at you to get your butt out of the middle of the road), languidly arise and mosey to the curb.

How to Release Tuna from the Impenetrable Can of Confinement

Canned tuna is like a caged bird—it longs to be set free. There's only one way to deal with trapped tuna. Make sure to follow all the steps outlined below.

1. Meow frantically.

2. When your human enters kitchen and says, "What? Do you want to be fed?" do your best "dead cat" impersonation at his or her feet to demonstrate how weak you've become from lack of protein.

3. While the can is being opened, be on the lookout for the dog, as most dogs are not smart enough to distinguish their food from yours.

4. Attempt to trip your human as he or she carries the food dish in order to have the food reach the floor that much sooner.

5. Plunge headfirst into tuna delight and eat until you feel the need to puke. (Or until you do puke. Whatever.)

6. Repeat.

What to Do if You're Left Outside in the Rain

If you're caught in a downpour, your first goal is always to get someone's attention. Try sitting outside a front door and wailing until someone opens up. If no one is home, crawl into a shed or garage or take refuge under the house, plotting your revenge as you wait out the storm.

How to Survive the Holiday Photo Shoot

If your neighborhood cat buddies ever caught sight of you in your elf suit knitted by Aunt Nan, your rep as the neighborhood bad boy would be destroyed. Here are some tricks to discourage the "family pet on holiday card" trend.

- Attack anyone who attempts to fasten a Santa hat, elf ears, or reindeer antlers on any part of your head or body.

- Hide deep inside the Christmas tree.

- Release a wave of kitty gas strong enough to wilt the poinsettias during the photo shoot.

Which Is Your Worst Case . . .
Birds outside the window or squirrels inside the walls?

- If a professional photographer is involved, steer that person toward a new career. Bonus points if you manage to vomit in the middle of a shoot.

- If all else fails, make sure your family is left with no choice but to pen, "Bah, humbug," beneath your photo before sending it out.

How to Survive the Vacuum Cleaner

A cat has many natural enemies—rocking chairs, baths, the vet tech who trims our nails, and, of course, vacuum cleaners. These cat-hair-sucking mistakes of nature represent a danger to every feline household. Stay calm, don't panic, and follow these guidelines.

HISS AND SPIT
The moment you spy the vacuum, make no bones about the fact that you consider it your mortal enemy. Sometimes this scares it into another room.

MOVE TO HIGHER GROUND
For whatever reason, vacuums seem reluctant to scale the refrigerator or dining room table. Use this to your advantage and climb.

GO DEEP
If you can't go high, seek out a nook or cranny into which you may cram yourself. Vacuums appear to prefer wide-open spaces and will often overlook corners or the spot way back under the bed. Warning: If suction tools are involved, abort this strategy

Which Is Your Worst Case . . .

Vacuum cleaner or doorbell?

instantly. There have been reports of felines being forced to endure head-to-toe suctioning with some of these nefarious devices.

RUN AWAY

It's the rare vacuum that can catch a cat. If cornered, tuck your tail between your legs, flatten your ears, and get yourself out of there.

How to Disappear

Despite being creatures who are often accused of being underfoot, cats also possess the skill of disappearing when the situation warrants. (Say, for example, when a glass of water decides to spontaneously spill all over the computer.) We suggest the David Copperfield method. Lie belly down on the floor while you intone, "Presto blendo, presto blendo . . ." People will walk right by.

How to Catch a Mouse

For many of us, domestic life has meant a lessening of our natural predator skills. Just because you live a life of refinement, however, doesn't mean you can't still hang a mounted mouse head on your wall, if you so choose. For cats who haven't had to stalk for survival, here's a brief refresher.

OLD SCHOOL

1. *Surveillance.* Post a twenty-four-hour (minus nap and feeding time) watch on the area where you suspect a mouse of habitating. If you have access to video monitoring devices, all the better.

2. *Surprise.* Practice the art of stillness. Even when the mouse appears, don't rush your pursuit. Allow the mouse to venture away from her hole.

3. *Engage bogey.* There's no need to lock on target and destroy with the first strike. Mousing is like fishing. You catch something solely in order to be able to thump your chest with pride and take a photo of you with your kill. Then you throw it back and attempt to catch it all over again.

NEW SCHOOL
Extend a formal dinner invite to the mouse, neglecting to mention what will be served as the main course.

How to Avoid Taking Medication

The important thing to remember with medication is that you must avoid ingesting it at all costs. No matter what you're told, anything that doesn't smell like fish, chicken, or butt can't be good for you.

THE FAKEOUT
Pretend to take the pill, hide it under your tongue or in the back of your throat, and then spit it out in the middle of the hall in full view of your humans once you've been released.

Which Is Your Worst Case . . .
Cross-country car ride or airplane cargo hold?

THE CHOKE

Many humans (rightfully) fear giving a cat a pill. Expand on this and make choking, gasping noises that panic your human into thinking you're hurt, allowing you time to escape.

WILD KITTY

Channel the raw, savage power of your ancestors. They used to eat people, you know.

How to Avoid Being Punished for Anything, Ever

You're a good kitty—most of the time. For those times when your halo might waver, it's good to know how to lay the blame at someone else's feet.

PULL BIG KITTY EYES

When you're in deep, pull out the big guns. Open your eyes as wide as possible, wriggle your nose, and purr. Nine times out of ten, people will instantly forget whatever it was they were upset about.

INVOLVE THE DOG

This ploy is so easy it's almost cruel. Lead the puppy to the (fill in the blank—broken dish, tilled plant, chewed shoe, crashed computer) and invite him to play. Wipe any incriminating cat paw prints from the scene with your tail and assume the "I'm as shocked by this behavior as you are" look when your human enters the room and sees Scout happily rolling in plant dirt.

BONUS CHAPTER

The Secret

All cats know the secret to life.

But we're not telling.

About the Author

DENA HARRIS has been a humor columnist for *Cats & Kittens* magazine and contributor to *Chicken Soup for the Soul: What I Learned from the Cat, Cup of Comfort for Cat Lovers, Chicken Soup for the Cat-Lover's Soul*, and *Chicken Soup for the American Idol Soul*. She is the author of *Lessons in Stalking* and *For the Love of Cats*. The host of her own monthly AM radio show and founder of a corporate communications company, Write for You, Dena lives in Madison, North Carolina, with her husband and two cats, Lucy and Olivia.

Index